DUM DUM CASTLE

YASIN AZIZ

Dum Dum Castle
by Yasin Aziz

Published as an ebook by Yasin Aziz June 2014

Table of Contents

2

About This Book

There is a well-documented historical account of a long battle in 1609–10 between Kurds and the Safavid Empire. The battle took place around a fortress called Dimdim, located in the Beradost region, near Lake Urmia in north-western Iran. In 1609, the ruined structure was rebuilt by Emîr Xan Lepzêrîn (Golden Hand Khan), ruler of Beradost, who sought to maintain the independence of his expanding principality in the face of both Ottoman and Safavid penetration into the region. Rebuilding Dimdim was considered a move towards independence that could threaten Safavid power in the northwest. Many Kurds, including the rulers of Mukriyan (Mahabad), rallied around Amir Khan. After a long and bloody siege led by the Safavid grand vizier Hatem Beg, which lasted from November 1609 to the summer of 1610, Dimdim was captured. All the defenders were massacred. Shah Abbas ordered a general massacre in Beradost, and Mukriyan (reported by Eskandar Beg Turkoman,

3

Safavid historian, in the book *Alam Aray-e Abbasi*) resettled the Turkish Afshar tribe in the region while deporting many Kurdish tribes to Khorasan. Although Persian historians (like Eskandar Beg) depicted the first battle of Dimdim as a result of Kurdish mutiny or treason, in Kurdish oral traditions (*Beytî dimdim*), literary works (Dzhalilov, pp 67–72) and histories, it was treated as a struggle of the Kurdish people against foreign domination. In fact, *Beytî dimdim* is considered a national epic second only to *Mem û Zîn* by Ahmad Khani. The first literary account of the Dimdim battle was written by Faqi Tayran.

About the Author

Yasin Mahmoud Aziz is from the town of Halabja in south Kurdistan. He came to England in late 1984, having been called to join Saddam's army in the fight against Iran. With no other way to avoid the war, he left the country, living in Bulgaria, working in Libya and Italy, and at last settling in England. As his English was poor, he attended college, where he studied for GCSEs, and went into higher education at the West London College / Brunel University to complete an honours degree in Business and Art. This was in 1996. He started work with the college's computer system, acting in maintenance and user support. A year later he was working as a civil servant with the Inland Revenue, and continued in that role for about ten years.

He has always tried to improve his English, especially as the mother of his two boys, his ex-wife, is English. He keeps fit, and has run over twenty-five marathons, a discipline that helps him to get over his homesickness and thoughts of troubles back home.

As soon as he'd begun to master English he started to write his book about Dum Dum Castle, with reference to historical facts about this tragic event. The original story was by Areb Shamo, an Armenian or Russian writer, who about fifty years ago translated it into Kurdish. It tells of a tribe who rebuilt the castle in trying to preserve their pastoral way of life and defend themselves, which they did for many years until their tragic end in 1605 CE. Kurds in the Middle East have always striven to carry on their way of life, despite threats to their very existence by invading superpowers.

The present author has called on historical facts through a Kurdish historian and friend from Halabja, dating back to his time in Iran during the Kurdish mass exodus in 1991, and Saddam's brutal attempt to wipe out the Kurds in north Iraq. To him he's especially grateful. It has been a long process, to write as a sort of historical novel events surrounding the Safavid and Ottoman empires, and conflict with the Persians. The aim has always been to bring to the English-speaking community a dramatisation of the history and struggle of the Kurds.

Yasin Aziz published two books in Kurdish in 2012, *Health & Fitness in Running Marathons*, and a book about well-known Kurdish personalities and poets from Islam's Middle Ages. Another book, about Saladin Ayubi as a Kurdish historical leader, and the Crusaders, is to be published soon, as will a book about the history of English poetry in Kurdish. Also planned are two more books in English on Kurdish poetry in Middle Ages Islam, and one with the working title *A Few Days in the Life of the Revolution in Halabja*, the town that was bombed with weapons of mass destruction in 1988 by Saddam. There are also poems published in England, some in translation, and reviews and articles published online, on various English and Kurdish topics.

Acknowledgements

Many thanks to Jane Tatam (my agent / consultant), my Editor Peter Cowlam, my friend and teacher the Kurdish historian Feiroz Hasan, my good friend Tony Cranston, who is the author of many children's books and a story teller who encouraged me with his wise direction and advice.

My book is dedicated to my sons Zardi and Surein.

Introduction

Historical background

The Kurds have a long history of struggle in the preservation of their tradition, culture and way of life. No one in the region has fought the Arabs' huge armies more than the Kurds in resisting conversion to Islam. It took the Arabs two years to conquer Kurdistan. In the following centuries the Kurds followed the same principle, fighting back against all potential occupiers.

For centuries, the impact of occupying powers hasn't been as great on the Kurds as on other, neighbouring nations, such as the Persians, Turks, Arabs and Armenians. That is probably best exemplified by the fact that Kurdish national costume is the same as it was almost 3,000 years ago. Nawroz, the Zoroastrian seventh feast, has been celebrated in Kurdistan and Persia ever since. The food and traditional way of life are almost as in Zoroastrian times, especially in the mountain villages.

9

The language is well preserved, and hasn't changed as much as that of other nations of the Middle East: Syria, Lebanon, Egypt, the Jordan valley and Iran. Over few centuries most of them were Arabised through conversion to Islam. It took 200 years for the people of Egypt to speak Arabic, but the Kurdish language has remained throughout.

The epic of Dum Dum Castle is one highlight from a struggle that has been active for centuries. What happened to an entire community, like many other facts, has been ignored by subsequent regimes, in an attempt to stamp out any historical exploration of the Kurds.

The tragedy of Dum Dum Castle is that, on its capture by the Safavid Army, half a million people were deported to Khuzestan in eastern Iran. Descendants of the castle people have led a Kurdish way of life in the midst of Persian culture ever since.

Kurdistan is located in western Asia, occupying a vast part of eastern Anatolia, right up to Armenia, northern Mesopotamia (Iraq), eastern Syria and western Iran. Its wealth of natural resources has tempted conquering powers since the first millennium BCE, and for that reason Kurdistan has been turned into a battleground. One of the very first power struggles was in the Assyrian period, 911–612 BCE.[FN1] The Kurds' only option was to fight back and resist, building citadels and sometimes withdrawing to the high rugged mountains for protection. [FN2]

Kurds are descendants of the Medes, who joined forces to end Assyrian incursion and the collection of taxes on the Kurds. Assyrian reign was finally ended when Nineveh, the Assyrian capital, was burned in 612 BCE. The Kurds founded an empire for nearly four centuries, with their capital Akbatana, or the city of Hamadan in Iran. Persians took over from the Medes through intermarriage and treachery. King Kurash put an end to the Kurds' Mede empire when he won a battle with the last Mede emperor, Astyages, and the Persian Empire was established.[FN3]

The events of Dum Dum Castle occurred in the era of Shah Abbas,[FN4] a ruthless Safavid ruler, with the Safavid Empire lasting from 1502 to 1722.[FN5]

11

Dum Dum Castle, known to have been built in the earlier Sassanid period, required rebuilding in the second half of the sixteenth century, when it was destroyed. According to the original narrator, Shah Abbas's brutality was directed not only at the Kurds but at all his enemies, even those included in his own family: he killed his own sons, Sofi Mirza and Muhamad Mirza, because of their growing power and popularity. His two other kinsmen, Khuda Qulley Mirza and Khuda Banda Mirza, were blinded under torture. His ruthlessness paralleled that of his predecessor Shah Ismael, 1500–1524 BCE, whose barbaric behaviour was incited by religious extremism, and directed against his opponents.

Here is a brief account of the foundation of the castle, according to *Aalam Arai Abbas*, written by Shah Abbas's biographer and historian, Askander Beig. Amir Khan, the head of the Bradoust Kurdish tribe, the biggest Kurdish tribe in the area, founded Dum Dum Castle in about the mid-sixteenth century. This happened after the Bradoust were forced to flee their lands and properties, from the other side of the border close to Lake Van in north Kurdistan and southeast Turkey. They were persecuted by the Ottoman Empire, and settled on the other side of the border inside the Safavid Empire, between Lake Van and Lake Urmia. Amir Khan was one of the most favoured Kurdish princes in Kurdistan – he gained the respect of the Persian Empire in the early days of the castle.

The Safavid era started with the victory of Shah Ismael over Aq quyunlu (the Turkish leader at that time), after which Ismael ascended to the throne and took the title of Shah, establishing his empire in Tabriz in 1501. The Safavids descended from the mystical Shaikh Saif al Din Ishaq in the city of Ardabil, 1252–1334, the time of the Mongol Empire's eleventh Khan. His teacher Taj al din Ibrahim Gilani Shaikh Zahid founded his own order in Ardabil.

The Safaviyya, protector of the poor and the weak, founded his convent in Ardabil. Ismael Shah installed the Shiite creed as the state religion, directly in line of Imam Ali (the cousin of the prophet

Muhammad).^{FN6}

Shah Abbas's policy towards the Kurds (1587–1629 CE) can be characterised by Askander Beig, historian and biographer, who said: 'Nothing could avert the danger of these bad and wretched people but the blade of the sword.' On the massacre of the many people of the castle by the Safavid Army, he added: 'They received their fair punishment and what they deserved.'

Notes

1 I M Diyakonov, *History of Med or Madde*, translated into Persian by Karim Shawerz, Tehran, p231.

2 Ahmed Jamal Rasheed, *Kurdish Studies on Suparto Land*, p38, Baghdad, 1984.

3 I M Dyakonov, *The History of Med or Madde*.

4 *Economics and Politics During the Safavid Empire*, Tehran, 1348 (Iranian calendar).

5 N A Musa, *Iraq in the Ottoman Era, 1700–1800 BC*, pp21–30, Baghdad, 1972.

6 Richard Frye, *The Golden Age of Persia*, p209,

Cambridge University Press, 1975.

Chapter One

The green terraced fields nestled in a bowl of high, snow-streaked mountains with a stream running through. Above the town rose a rusty purple fortress, the Dum Dum Castle. The castle and its community were huddled at the waist of a high chain of mountains, with their rocky tips and sharp cliffs. The castle community consisted of about 400 people, with roughly 100 families in all, a population added to by the surrounding villages. Swelling those numbers also were the castle's warriors.

It was situated on a largely flat expanse, partitioned by a sixty-foot-high stone wall, which was twenty feet thick, and held together with clay. The castle's two walnut doors opened on a pair of spiralling roads deep into the valley below.

Thick green woodland was a cover on these two roads. The castle's five main towers were guarded round the clock. The surrounding region was mostly mountainous – between the mountains narrow stretches of arable plains were used for field crops and vegetables, and orchards lined the terraces to the foot of the castle. Livestock were scattered on the plains' rich pastures, but in summer most of the herds grazed on the mountain slopes.

A river gushed down from the northeast, close to the north side of the castle, where it was partly diverted to serve its inhabitants. Fresh sparkling water flowed through the two main ditches, where streams of water branched out to Khanu's divan, the mosque, the houses, the local manufacturers, the pond in the market, and, the final destination, the mill, before reconciliation with the main stream down in the valley. Its supply kept the castle fresh and green even in summer, when rain stopped for nearly six months.

A great many mulberry trees, willows, oaks, chinnars (a tall slim tree), walnuts and a variety of bushes, roses and shrubs, were watered and well looked after by the castle people.

Khanu's two-storey divan and the mosque were the main landmarks of the castle town. The divan's two ornamented domes with their yellow, navy and turquoise tiles stood out, and were separated by a wooden balcony on which were two rows of columns that overlooked the market square.

In early spring the high slopes of the surrounding mountains were still covered with snow, which did not disappear until well into the middle of summer. It was an early spring morning.

The people were beginning to come out from their winter shelters to dig and plough their allotments situated round their houses, and work in their orchards. They came to sow vegetable seeds, an activity they called 'spring sowing'. The image of winter was not yet far from people's minds.

A dark bank of cloud above the northern mountains lingered, but winter was dismissed with a rambling, roaring, lightning and thunder, followed by torrential rain, transforming the dust to soil.

Whenever this happened the rain soon cleared, leaving a moistness in the soil, which in turn gave way to a piercing sun. The newly ploughed soil scented the spring air. The rain was called 'goorga zie' (meaning the season of wolves giving birth).

In the following weeks excessive spring rain, and snow melted from the mountain slopes and ravines, caused the river to overflow, surging down, cascading and rumbling over rock piles, its foam and froth able to bring down rocks with a deafening roar. This could be frightening.

This was the contradiction to the river's sparkling, diamond look in its quiet summer mood, as it often seemed as it passed beneath the castle, solemn in its gratitude. Dazzling shoals of iridescent fish could always be seen swimming in the river.

It wasn't long before the orchards were bouncing with white blossom, set off against the greenness of the leaves, and clusters of buds sprang into the freshness of early spring and the warmth of its sunshine.

Each afternoon water overflowed the brims of the banks, often flooding the mill, though at night the miller had no such worry, as the drop in temperature slowed the melting of the snow. During the day he laid out piles of rocks to divert the water, so as not to overwhelm his mill.

In early spring he was busy clearing the ditches, pruning branches and preparing an appropriate mill-stone, in order to make the best fine flour for the castle people.

Khursheed, the 'town inspector', often sent men to assist the miller, and to clear the ditches. Early spring was the beginning of the Kurdish new year, and the castle was crowded with villagers, farmers and traders, who came to sell their livestock, to exchange products, to shop and to see relatives, kinsmen and friends.

People from as far as Azerbaijan, Tabriz, Erzroum and Wan were seen around the castle, with bargaining seen everywhere. 'Come here, brother! Come! Here, brother, come! Here you'll find the best bargains you can get.' People were selling animal oil, kashk (clots of yoghurt in little bits and dried in summer, which are softened overnight with water and eaten with warm bread and sweet tea for breakfast), various types of cheese, nuts, grains, etc....

Some were selling materials ready made into men's wear – traditional Kurdish costume – with head scarves of silk or cotton, leather jackets, belts, pastak and faranji (waistcoats locally made from wool or goat's hair.) A few shops were selling women's hats, ornamented with coloured beads, stones and silver. Women's cummerbunds were made of leather or wool and prettied with loops of silver, and there were earrings, bracelets and chains.

There was a teashop in the castle market, where people sat and chatted in the sunshine on wooden benches and chairs, in the shade of the trees. Some sat in the shacks, with tea or coffee or with light snacks consisting of dairy products – butter, cheese, yoghurt.

In summer, the most popular meal was yoghurt and dou (a yoghurt drink made after separating the butter from the yoghurt), which was taken with fresh homemade bread and green vegetable herbs.

There were a few regular comers, and old people who narrated stories of the 'good old days', peppered with tales of their experience and adventures, and with religious thoughts and poetry.

Askander, usually known as Eskow, was a well-known elder, often seen at the teashop. He was one of the regulars, distinguished by the wounds of many battles. He had a slight hunchback and a scar to his left eyebrow. Whenever in the mood to talk, he sipped his coffee and blinked, which stretched his scar just slightly.

Wounds he'd got were in wars in defence of his country. 'The story I'm about to tell happened a long time ago,' he said, 'when I was young and naïve. I used to be a strong and well-built youth!' He looked around where the young men were sitting and listening attentively. 'I spent a few years with the Khalidian Amir, as their peasant, when they had long-term animosity with the Mllad tribe. For many years they were fighting one another. The Diyarbakr governor was always backing the Mllads, stirring their animosity in one way or another.'

He slurped his coffee and paused, thinking and looking far ahead at the horizon. Then he started again: 'Once there was a rumour that the Turks were coming to Kurdistan to collect taxes, that they had sent an army led by Shuker Pasha, the governor of the area, to subvert the Kurds. The Kurds refused to pay taxes, as they often did. Rumour spread rapidly. The tribes began preparations to repel Shuker Pasha's army.

The Turks began attacking villages – even when the relationship between our two tribes was bad, we soon went to their assistance to drive the Turks out. In the meantime, our leader, Murad Khan, received a letter from the Kurdish Mir of Van supporting our stand: "Let's get together, and join forces to repulse the Turks. We should forget past animosity, which anyway was stirred by the interfering Ottomans, through the governor of Diyarbakr."

It was quite obvious that the Turkish army was killing indiscriminately: unarmed civilians, the old, women and children. Who could see that and not stand up and fight? It didn't take more than a week to ready our warriors, who were led by the Mir's brother Zorow Beig. He was well known for his chivalry. I remember that once Zorow said, "Gallantry alone is not sufficient for a true fighter; it is crucial one uses tactics, is scrupulous and is deceitful in defeating the enemy.'"

He stopped to wrap some tobacco.

'I often saw him fight. What he used to do was not stage his attacks specifically in one direction or stay in one place, but hit and run, so it was difficult for the enemy to retaliate. Once during a fight, I suddenly found myself among some Turks. I killed two of them, but the third almost chopped my head off: when I raised my shield to protect my head, his sword clipped my shield and halved my left ear – but I didn't let him get away with it. I put my sword through his heart. That is why I'm here now, still alive, but a blow to my left shoulder has left me with joint pain that flares in the cold of winter.'

With a boastful smile, he was about to start again, but one of the listeners suddenly interrupted. 'Uncle Askander, did you all have horses or were some of you on mules or on foot?'

Askander, as if startled, and with a jerk of his head, turned to him. 'How can anyone fight like that without a horse? Without horses, how could we do hit and run? They would simply overrun us and slaughter all of us!' He screwed his stare at his listeners, and waited. Then he resumed.

'Their army withdrew, leaving many dead.' The

people who had gathered seemed very interested, no one uttering a word. When he'd finished he judged the time by the position of the sun and its light on the wall.

With the afternoon shadows approaching, it was time for afternoon prayer. 'Let's worship and refresh ourselves,' he said. It seemed he wanted everyone to follow him: he stood up, put his wrinkled hands to his waist and looked around, slowly walking out along the way. Most of his listeners followed, but there were a few young men who lingered behind, talking about his story and exchanging views.

Khursheed, the castle inspector, the man looking after the town, appeared from far away with his men on horses. It was quite clear from the shopkeepers' reactions, peering out from their shops with signals for each other, that his arrival was disapproved of and resented. His presence always meant something unpleasant and ominous.

He pulled up in the middle of the market, tugging the bridle of his horse so strongly that its hooves sprung into the air. Without getting off, and with his thick moustache twitching upwards, almost covering his nostrils, and frowning under bushy eyebrows, he roared with anger: 'I told you two days ago! It's now spring. You have to clean up the ditches before they stink. Why is that not done yet?' He shouted at the top of his voice.

No one dared utter a word, as he started again: 'I give you three more days. I swear to God, if they're not cleared, I'll put a heavy fine on every one of you! A hundred lashes each, I'm warning you, and don't tell me later I have no fear of God or have been unfair!' He shouted so loudly that the shopkeepers came out to see what the commotion was.

He galloped off with his men, heading towards the local craftsmen: blacksmiths, carpenters, etc. These were situated 200 yards further west, having settled with their families just behind the shops. The road to the market passed in front of these shops, two rows of them, connected to houses at the back. At the front were benches of wood or flat stones, and a display of their wares – handmade wood, copper and iron products, also porcelain, pottery and basketwork, pans, bowls and wooden cutlery.

There was a shop for glossing copper saucepans, and for cleaning and whitening plates with enamel, as a protection against rust. The carpenters made cradles, boxes for clothes, sieves, spoons, plates, candy-containers, trays and other household wares. Baskets were woven from straw and from soft, strong brushwood.

The blacksmith's was one of the most attractive scenes of all. In it was a small fireplace, whose rising flames made the air inside the hut hot all day. The place vibrated with the deafening noise of hammers, and was filled with scrap metal: the remains of axes, machetes, hammers, scythes, ploughs, sickles, hoes, rakes, chains, swords, shields, and numerous other objects. The interior was dark from soot and filled with smoke, which drifted up into the outside.

Apprentices pumped air into the furnace, with

folding leather bags, until hot enough to soften the metal shafts, for hammering and moulding into the required shapes. There was a smell of sweaty clothes, and burning paint as it peeled from the metal, and a careworn look on the faces of the workmen. There were three in all, the master and his two apprentices, in tattered, threadbare clothes.

They would jump up on to the forge one after another, the master shouting out to the rest to tell them where to strike with their tools. The finished products proved the virtue of a man's grip on nature, demonstrated through such simple discipline. People in the neighbouring houses and shops were drilled by the blacksmith's monotonous rhythm, as an almost mythical force.

When Khursheed came round, there was still ash from the day before. The scene irritated him so much he started shouting. 'You! Pumpkin heads! How many times did I tell you to clean and tidy up? How long do you expect me to overlook your ignorance?'

With these remonstrations he whipped one of the apprentices, as an example to the others, then asked his men to take him to the castle.

Dum Dum Castle was not as big as other towns, but still one could find whatever one could think of. People came from all around, to shop or barter. The castle had a cattle market, which was a small open area spared for livestock, horses, donkeys, mules, firewood and the coal trade.

The tribes of Bradoust lived in the area around the castle, in Azerbaijan as it used to be called. Tabriz, the Temorid capital city, used to be one of the largest towns near the castle, as was the Kurdish town of Urmeya. (As Thevenost, the French traveller, wrote in the sixteenth and seventeenth centuries, Azerbaijan was like a caravansary: merchants travelled in from all directions, routes crisscrossing the Azerbaijan-Kurdistan plateau, which linked the East and West, central Asia, India, Russia and China to Europe.)

Caravans carried merchandise in from Syria bound for Turkey. Goods of all kinds were sold – cotton materials, clothes, carpets, taffetas, raw silk, jewellery and women's perfumes. Goods came from Sultanyia and Tabriz, the main merchant centres of the region. Spices numbered cloves, nutmeg, cinnamon, manna, mace and other Indian specialities.

Silk was imported from Gailan, with other goods from Yazd, Shiraz, Samarkand, Bukhara, Tartary and China. Precious stones and pearls came via the port of Hormuz from Africa and India. Large caravans of 800 camels came from China to Tabriz and Azerbaijan, taking six months to arrive. Erzroum was one of the greatest cities in northern Kurdistan, and was known as one of the greatest commercial cities, no lesser in importance than Qazvin and Tabriz. Yazd and Kashan were known for their fine carpet manufacture.

In the castle market people sold sheep, goats, cattle, horses, mules, donkeys and game – partridges, quails, wood pigeons, hares. People came from far away to buy horses, their good qualities summarised in short, erect ears, wide, high chests, relatively small heads, slim, strong limbs, and they were valued as working animals able to travel for days without exhaustion. They were used to a rugged, mountainous landscape.

The market dealt in household products too: beads, buttons, needles, threads, laces, hats, silks and headscarves. Merchants came with materials for clothing. One of the small kiosks had lentil soup, from a recipe including the meaty bones of sheep, goats and veal. Heads of lambs and sheep-stomach skins were stuffed with herbs and rice.

There were other dishes, such as kaurma (skinless wheat boiled and cooked with meaty bones). The attendants were traders, peasants, shepherds and summer labourers. Some did all kinds of work: selling wood cut from the mountain forest, and used for winter fuel, while others made and sold charcoal.

In summer there was a greater variety of jobs:

farming; the harvesting of wheat and barley, fruit picking, fruit and vegetable drying, juice- and sweet-making (basook), using grape juice thickened and hardened with flour.

There was a syrup made from pomegranate and other fruit. In autumn, gazo (a syrup-like tree sap collected from oak-tree leaves) was collected and purified and dried into lumps, and sold. The summertime too saw the selling of piles of snow, accumulated in mountain bunkers.

They were dug up and loaded onto mules, and sawn into lumps and broken up for sale as drinking water, with yoghurt and various juices.

Kursheed, the market inspector, was heading towards Musa's house near the local craftsmen, opposite the food house belonging to a man from the Jezira region, named Bahadeen. He, as soon as he saw Kursheed on his horse, rushed out to greet him, asking him with utmost politeness to get off. 'I have just finished scorching some sliced lean lamb on saj [a round, smooth piece of metal heated up and used for making bread and scorching meat]. You must be very hungry. You're very busy, inspecting the market; please help yourself to some of this freshly cooked meat.' He invited Khursheed inside.

Khursheed said nothing about the mess and dirt and buzzing flies, more concerned with filling his stomach. An assistant rushed out to help him with his horse as he got off.

Every now and again he flashed the lamb down with a bowl of Sultana's cool drink. When he'd finished he thanked God, 'alhamdu leillah'. Only after his feast did he again get ready to hassle the traders and shopkeepers. However, today he seemed to be going in a different direction, to a cave round the back of the castle, where a craftsman was staying, who'd arrived from near Van. (Van is an ancient town in the Ottoman area in northern Kurdistan.)

Nariman, the master craftsman, and an ex-army

commander, had come to manufacture weapons for the castle's defence. Nobody was allowed to enter the cave apart from Khanu's men. Khursheed left his horse and his men outside and entered the cave. Nariman, who was a tall, well-built man, instantly came forward to greet him.

'Oh my dear friend! I'm so pleased to see you. Khanu asked me to talk to you; to enquire about anything you may require,' Khursheed immediately informed this newly arrived guest. He stretched out a hand to shake Nariman's and added the other for emphasis.

'God protect our leader Khanu, for giving us hope to stand up to our enemies, and God protect him and his men. I'm pleased to meet you and to be here, sir,' replied Nariman.

'I'm at your service, sir. I've been sent to invite you to Khanu's divan tomorrow for lunch,' Khursheed replied to the master, still clasping his hands.

'Thank you very much, God protect our Khanu. I'm so grateful to Khanu for honouring me with his care and respect. I would be humbled to see him at his divan. And, after all, it is very important for me to see him myself, and personally tell him what I need,' Nariman said.

Khursheed left, though he promised to come back with a horse in due time and take Nariman to the divan. He stopped, however, on hearing the clink of a caravan coming up behind him. He ordered his men to stop too.

The sound seemed to please him, as he knew he was soon to receive gifts. Although Khanu had forbidden the taking of baksheesh (money or presents) from foreign caravans, Khursheed still did so in secret. He didn't take from all of them, but only from ones he knew, for fear of discovery and punishment by Khanu.

He was heading towards the castle gate where ten mules with trunks and men were waiting. At the head of the caravan an old man with a white beard and a sallow face sat on a grey horse. He wore a plain white tunic, which fluttered in the mountain breeze, and had a cloak spread over his shoulders.

There was a double black ring resting on his head, with a loose, thin headscarf, also white. He was puffing on his pipe, with a hand to the bridle. The single guard of the castle didn't speak Arabic. He called for an interpreter.

As soon as Khursheed reached the gate, he went to the Arab, shouting as he approached. 'Marhaba, uncle,' Khursheed said, greeting him with a smile. The man dismounted, and shook Khursheed's hand in returning the greeting.

Khursheed spoke very good Arabic – he had dealt with many Arabs before. 'My name is Marwan and I come from Sham [Syria]. I heard about this castle and always wished to come here. I have also heard about Khanui Lap Zereen, who is known for his generosity and fairness. It is he who has secured peace and stability in this region. I will, enshallah [if god is willing], come back more often.'

As Khursheed heard this, he nodded with a welcome smile. 'You are very welcome, Uncle Marwan!' he said. After the routine inspection of his trunks, Marwan was let in. He looked immediately to the town. At first, the Arab merchant had mistaken Khursheed for Khanu, and had greeted him as such. 'I am honoured, and am very pleased to see your great castle.'

Khursheed explained with a smile that he was the castle inspector, not Khanu. 'Khanu is very kind and hospitable, especially with honest guests,' he said, then ordered one of his men to show the way to Musa's rest house. There Marwan was received with respect and shown to his lodge.

The room was ready: the fire was lit, and the floor carpeted with mats and rugs. There was a single mattress. The horses were brought to the forecourt and their loads taken off before they were stabled. The rest of the men were shown a spacious room.

It was nearly midday when Khursheed was going home for lunch. He deliberately chose the alleyway, where Maksood's house was located, in order to catch a glimpse of his daughter Dilbar. He was lucky enough to see her, as she was putting out and dusting rugs and carpets, using a wooden pole and a straw brush, and basking in the sunshine. She was in a good mood; it was early spring.

She wasn't aware of his presence, but *he* was delighted with her. He started twitching his moustache, a sure sign of anxiety and anticipation, and took off his turban. He rearranged it on his head and raised his voice, talking to his men, ostensibly.

Kursheed had been married several times and already had two wives, but now he had set his sights on Dilbar. She was in her late teens, pretty and agile. Many times Khursheed had sent men to ask her father for her hand in marriage, but he always refused. He sent her presents, rare bracelets and necklaces got from foreign merchants, but every time she promptly sent them back. Still, he wouldn't give up.

'Khursheed already has two wives. I wouldn't let him take Dilbar,' her father always said.

Dilbar might have been considered a fairy princess of the castle: her dark brown eyes; her tall, slender figure; her Caucasian complexion; her rosy cheeks, and on the lower left a black mole; in short, she had glamour. She was well known for these good looks. Many a young man would have been grateful to make her his wife, but she turned them all down – perhaps with someone special in mind.

She never masqueraded, and didn't wear make-up; she acted as naturally as possible, and her taste in dress was unique, her two dark plaits almost reaching her waist, ornamented with silver jewels. She liked to wear colourful waistcoats with gold or silver edgings, coloured beads and dark precious stones, and with anklets with looping silver rings. She wore a silver cummerbund, which she left loose on her hip.

She had a thin cap sewn with beads and laces, and stitched with silver chains, which as it glittered in the sunshine looked like a crown. It was wrapped with silk a light blue, green and maroon. She had a silver ring in her nose, a fine light loop, and she wore a pair of traditional leather shoes embroidered with yellow, green and red.

They had sharp, soft tips bent upwards, and were called Paniberz. When she saw Khursheed, she turned her back on him, but Kursheed took no notice. He was used to being ignored.

As he approached her his voice became a whisper:

'My sweetheart, even when you turn away from me,
   I still think that you're my prey.
   You cannot escape, you will be mine one day.
   I will get you and you will become my wife,

I will keep you like a princess in the castle of my heart, for life.'

Dilbar, annoyed at his recitation, turned to Khursheed, and looked straight into his eyes. 'You are so very unjust, and read everything amiss. You've two at home already...waiting for you,' she said angrily.

'Another nibble isn't too much, don't you think? Koran has made it halal,' Kursheed grunted in an undertone.

'Go away!

For all your greedy jaw and lust,
you will never get a hold of me,
for I am not your easy prey!'

Khursheed could not contain his irritation: 'I swear to God – I will get you, either by money or force. I will do whatever it takes!' He was angry and frowning.

'That is but a dream, for who do you think you

are? It's only your illusion: you think you can take any woman you like. You are a fool! You should remember, I have four brothers who would skin you like a fox! Don't be so stupid. Be reasonable.' Dilbar turned away and slammed the door.

She had been in love with Shebab, Addi's son, for a long time. They often met outside the castle, in the mountains, and took shelter behind the trees. They had sworn to belong to each other, as many were aware. Their parents knew too, but no one uttered a word – they were still so young. Their families saw them as for each other, as they were of the same tribe.

Chapter Two

The sun was setting, village fires were alight and smoke was rising lazily in the still air.

From the mosque's fifteen-foot-high minaret, in the far corner of the castle, was the best view of the surrounding chain of mountains. Master Nadir, who had just finished building the minaret, was showing it to Khanu, the vault being its most prominent feature, and a thing of great beauty.

It was finished with navy blue and yellow tiles, and rounded with a two-foot-high circular brick wall at mid-height. It was edged at the brim with jagged maroon and yellow tiles, where the mullah went for the call to prayer.

Khanu, impressed with the end product, asked the Master Nadir for an opinion on the castle towers. The problem was Shah Abbas's animosity towards Khanu, especially as Shah was Shiite and Khanu was Sunni. There was a need to maintain Khanu's authority, with Shah Abbas intent on subjugating him

44

and his people. They discussed a plan for the renovation and strengthening of the towers, even stronger than Mardin Castle's.

In the morning, as usual, the call to prayer echoed in the valleys and mountains, summoning the faithful. Khanu was awake before dawn. His lodge was near water, and his space for prayer and his rug were in the mosque. Mullah Rasheed, who led prayers five times a day, was responsible for religious duties, events and teachings, with the help of his assistants.

Master Nadir, as Khanu's guest, accompanied Khanu at his morning prayer. When they were ready to leave, two of Khanu's men, who were waiting at the door, told him of two visitors here to see him. They had come from afar, by the looks of their horses, exhausted and laved with sweat. They were tired and did not seem to have slept. It was likely they were here to settle a tribal dispute, given the early hour.

They were armed. One was an emir, young, superior in his bearing, tall, well built, with an olive complexion, a straight nose and clear brown eyes. He wore a woollen beige scarf, and had a spear and a bow and arrows. With the latter went a beautifully ornamented brown leather quiver, slung on his horse. There was a curved rectangular shield on his shoulder, tied to his coat with laces and loops.

His khanjer (a dagger) was sheathed in his belt. It had a deer-horn handle and was embroidered with coloured beads – red, blue, silver. He looked ready for the battlefield.

The other was not as well equipped, though equally well built, tall, and armed with bow and arrows, a sword and a lance. He put these aside when he saw Khanu's men. Khanu, warrior-like, wore a brown leather vest, loose sharwal (Kurdish baggy trousers) and a light-brown jiba thrown over his shoulders (a jiba is a loose overall made from wool and embroidered with lace at the front). His own dagger had an ivory handle.

His face was broad face and of an olive complexion. He had soft hazel eyes, reddish brown hair and a thick moustache, trimmed and pointing upward. His dignified stature commanded his people's respect. He had given them stability. He greeted the young men. 'I hope nothing calamitous this early hour.'

In turn they took Khanu's hand and kneeled to kiss, paying their respect.

'We are from the Shikak tribe, sir. The Ottoman Army have been harassing us for the last two weeks, demanding taxes. They take anything they can get their hands on, even our rugs and quilts. Whoever refuses to pay they whip to death. If any villager shows resistance they take their cattle, their herds, and their homesteads are destroyed. Clan chiefs are stripped of their authority. We are sent to ask for your assistance, God protect our Khanu,' the young man said.

Khanu paused and looked grave. He could do nothing straightaway, preoccupied as he was with his towers, for which he had sent Khachow to Erzroum for iron grids and shafts. The visitors followed him to his divan, and from their manners Khanu could tell they were from the Shikak leader's family.

'The Ottomans and the Persians always encourage division and conflict,' Khanu said. 'If they don't succeed, they attack us. We must all join forces and unite.'

His guests agreed.

They reached home and had morning tea. Khanu sent for his elder son Saifaldin, and told him that the Shikak tribe were in difficulties: 'You must prepare 500 men and horse to go to fight the Turks.'

The two young men were delighted. 'Our great emir, may your reign prosper and your name exist for ever. God protect you for us, we are so grateful to you.'

In two days, the 500 horsemen were ready and

were on their way to rescue the Shikaks. Khanu's instructions were: 'Do not to face the Turkish Army head on. We don't know how many they are. Ambush them on the roads, in the woods and during the night. It must be hit and run, and you must show a willingness and stamina for the chase. It's a hunt rather than combat. When you get there, have plenty of rest. Attempt nothing till dawn.'

It took them three days to reach the Shikaks. They took breaks at six-hour interval, for food and rest, and attention to the horses. Villagers greeted them cordially, giving fresh bread, yoghurt and butter. On the eve of their attack they halted the regiment and remained in the mountains, hidden. They sent out two warriors to monitor the enemy's position. They were ready for a dawn attack.

That night a few warriors went to Saifaldin for permission to light a fire. They gathered wood in the moonlight, bright streaks spearing through the clouds. 'I'll start the fire,' Shebab said. He struck his flint on a stone, directing a shower of sparks onto some dry bark. It took time, but finally a tiny plume of smoke showed. Dropping to his belly, he blew gentle breaths over the tinder. A flame sprang up. His compatriot returned with sticks and branches, and in the next instant a group of warriors had a campfire to sit round.

It was three in the morning when they got ready to attack. Shebab woke up and moved to rouse everyone else. When they were ready and marching forward, Saifdin, the head of the cavaliers, addressed his men. 'Look, castle warriors, we are here to honour Khanu's pledge and assist our brothers. , We must give it everything we can.' He gave them orders to avoid the trodden track, so as to surprise the enemy. They galloped fast, with swords, spears and lances raised. They attacked from three sides, eager for vengeance. 'There can be no let off! Don't let them escape!' Saifdin was shouting.

Jozow grabbed a man by his shirt collar, hauling him in range of a savage head butt. Blood exploded

50

from the man's nose. He hurled him aside then slashed his sword in a wide arc. It struck a Turk in the forearm, slicing through his flesh and spraying blood. 'Come at me, would you?' On he raged, his sword hacking and slashing, left and right.

For a moment the enemies fell back from the fury of his assault. Then they surged forward, the huge form of Pestow on his right clattering in, spilling men to the ground. Then came Saifaldin, his sword stabbing out like a serpent's tongue, lancing into throats, chests and bellies. 'You are all dead men now!' Saifaldin bellowed.

A Turk darted at him, stabbing for the throat. Saifadin threw up his arm, his shield blocking the blow, cleaving his sword against the Turk's skull and shearing away his ear. The man screamed and fell back.

Other castle warriors joined in the fight. Shebab shoulder charged one, sending him flying. Saifaldin continued to rage at them, shouting battle cries and insults as he powered forward.

51

Jozow forced his way to the right of Saifaldin, who was fighting defensively, protecting those around him. He was tiring, for he fought with no economy of effort, slashing his sword with all his might. A Turk hurled himself at him, his club thudding against his leather breastplate.

Saifaldin stumbled and fell back to the ground. Shebab turned swiftly, plunging his sword through the back of the Turk's neck. The dead man fell across Saifaldin's path. At this Shebab took up a defensive position, knowing Saifadin was too exhausted to block any further attack. He pushed the dead Turk away and slowly climbed to his feet, breathing deeply.

The noise of battle was all round him, and the stony ground was thick with blood. His sore arm felt as if weighed with rocks, but his strength was returning.

Surprised at the strength of this onslaught, the

Turks began to wane. There were no more drums and banners at their stations, many had fallen in the dust, others had escaped, and over fifty were captured, their weapons and rations seized, with Hassan Beig, their leader, killed.

'How many did we lose?' Saifaldin asked. Five dead and thirteen injured, five of them seriously. Thirty-three Turkish warriors were killed, with forty-two injured. Those captured were taken away for questioning and were later released, with a message for their leader.

'We the Kurds ask you to leave us alone. We ask to be left to manage our own affairs. We don't need you. We want nothing to do with you. We are all ready to fight back if you dare interfere in our lives or invade our land. If you were true Muslims, you would know that Muslims shouldn't kill each other. Be truthful to your God and leave us in peace.'

In his speech at the burial ceremony, he spoke of loyalty and courage, and he prayed to mighty God to guide their spirit along the path of judgement. He read verses of the departed, while silence fell over the gathering.

For the time being the Turkish Army and tax collectors were defeated, and the people jubilant and grateful to Khanu's warriors. The mood was festive, with Khanu's warriors invited by the Shikak leader for lunch at his divan. Other tribal chiefs visited, and invited them to their villages. The festivities lasted for a couple of days.

They lingered on their return home, hosted by tribal leaders who had heard of their success. They were praised and greeted with warm hospitality, and given gifts of handmade shoes, clothes and rugs.

Saifadin delivered Khanu's message to the villagers and tribal leaders: 'We must unite, support each other in the face of the Persian and Ottoman Empires, always our biggest threat.'

The tribes in their response promised warriors and financial aid for Khanu, as he had always been ready to assist them.

Chapter Three

The New Year festival, Nawroz, was just coming up
(21st March and the first day of the New Year), and
the people were busy with preparations, with sweets,
nuts and other edibles, and sherbet drinks. Some
made pastry, such as kulicha, paklava, zlubia and
others.

Festivities would usually begin on the evening of
the 20th, just after sunset. Bonfires were set up on
the high slopes of the mountains, and on the hills
around the towns and villages.
 The bigger the bonfire, the happier the crowd.
Everywhere, as far as one could see, was a blaze of
fires and a swirl of smoke.
People danced, young and old, accompanied by
dahol and zurna (traditional Kurdish musical
instruments). It was a time for the longings of lovers,
who clasped hands and joined in the dance.

Celebrations went on well into early morning, with folk singers, games and storytelling, and readings from Fakyea Tairans's *Twelve Cavaliers of Marivan*.

From daybreak everyone wished everyone else a happy Nawroz, while still the music played, its merriment attracting many from afar. The castle was filled with visitors. There were fortune-tellers and palm-readers, while magicians and the religious saw scope to make money.

That was especially so in the writing of *nushta*, for the protection of young people from evil and envious eyes. The palm-readers always had news of future lovers.

The young men were told to hide their *nushtas* in small holes in the ground near their lovers' houses, as that would magically open the girls' hearts. Some promised to do that straightaway, on the following evening or late at night. 'I swear I will do that tonight, and won't let anyone see me.' This was not only for young lovers. It could be used for couples who couldn't conceive, or for families who had no boys, or for the sick seeking recovery.

During the festival, the castle guard was warned to be on its mettle, as enemies could easily take advantage. The divan was thronged with guests – tribal leaders, Khanu's family, representatives of the Braduost and Shakak tribes. Veterans and merchants were also there, bearing gifts, in some cases a hundred sheep for Khanu.

'Khanu, you have saved us from the Persian Empire.'

Musa, the guesthouse owner, offered Khanu twenty pieces of gold. Three whole lambs were prepared for the grill, with seasoning and herbs, and served with rice, raisins, nuts, okra, fasolia, apricot and plums. Also for the grill were partridges and pheasants, wood pigeon and wild duck.

A sufra, or large rug, was spread with food and wooden plates, spoons and fresh leaves with sherbet and yoghurt drink.

The celebrations continued without a hitch, the guests and castle warriors treated to good food and lively entertainments. Then one of the organisers approached Khanu. 'Our great amir, the guards have arrested a stranger, who refuses to speak until he sees you.'

Khanu enquired as to his nationality, which was Kurdish. He told the guard to bring the stranger to him.

'Tell me who you are, young man. Speak up and don't waste my time!'

'Peace and grace of God be upon you, sir, our amir. I am honoured to meet you.' The man knelt down before Khanu.

Khanu put him at his ease, and sent him to somewhere to sit where food and drink were brought.

He was hungry, having not eaten for days.

'You obviously are a Kurd, and know the custom – first eat, then talk.' Khanu invited him to come forward and disclose the true purpose of his visit.

'My name is Hamza Chawesh, and I come from Mardin. I have been serving in the Ottoman Army for the last ten years. I have come to be at your service, our great amir.' The young man went on, 'I have trained many in the army. Senior officers say anyone who stands up for himself, and for his rights, is blasphemous and anti-Islam. Anyone who speaks out should be punished with utmost cruelty, and the punishment may apply to his family and the seizure of his properties.

I have been deceived by them. When they turn on my country and do the same to my people they use and exploit religion for their own interest. I could not stand it anymore. Now I come to serve my people, my country and Your Excellency.' He was desperate for someone to believe his story.

'It's a long time since I heard about you, sir. But it's as if my dream has come true. I am here to join your castle warriors. I plead with you, our great amir, to accept me as a warrior and as a faithful servant of my country. I hope I can be useful to you. I can train your men. I have experience with cavaliers and infantry in the use of weapons. Swords, lances, bow and arrow. I am well versed in battleground discipline.'

Khanu listened attentively. 'Young man, if you have come with sincere intentions, these people are your brothers and sisters. If I find you to be dishonest, I will have no mercy, and you will be punished. For now you are our guest.' Khanu studied his reaction.

He kissed Khanu's hand, and when led away was given clothes and weapons and allowed to join the castle regiment. He was to be under supervision until he had earned acceptance into the castle community.

He was introduced to the other warriors under the auspices of one of the senior guards. They came across Barruon, who was a well-known cavalier from the Tagur tribe, one strongly allied with Khanu's.

61

Barruon offered his blessings.

News of Hamza Chawesh spread among the villagers and young men who came for training. Hamza integrated well, giving a good impression of a hard-working young man, who showed his qualities in training, as he had said he would.

In the early June mornings, the harvest season, the heaths, meadows and plains were buzzing with noise, the farmers busy with barely and wheat. At this time, military training sessions were temporarily suspended, as help with the crops was the first necessity. When these sessions resumed, Hamza gathered his trainee conscripts behind the castle, and drilled them for the battlefield.

'You should all know that the cavalier regiment is always at the front. A cavalier must know how to control his horse. If a man cannot maintain his position and move confidently, he is easy prey for the enemy.' Hamza demonstrated the cavalier's manoeuvres, getting on his horse and starting to galloping. He altered his speed suddenly, swinging his sword over his head in great spectacle, but still glued to the saddle brought his horse to a standstill.

'Now it's your turn,' he said to one of his men.

He watched the young cavalier, and was soon pleased to see so many others doing so well, though there were still a few mistakes to iron out.

'We all learn from what we don't do right. Practice is the right way to perfection'.

They too a break with light snacks – bread, honey, walnut, butter, dried fruits, yoghurt drink. They shared whatever they had. In the following session Hamza gathered his men.

'Now we will learn how to manage in the battlefield with shields, swords and spears, and how to control the horses.' He divided his recruits into groups with different disciplines: cavaliers, archery, spears, shields, tactical, ambush.

In the days following there were schedules for building stamina – how to withstand thirst and hunger in the hours of summer heat. There were field exercises away from the castle, with the recruitment of village conscripts, on stand-by as reservists in time of war.

In late summer and early autumn, it was the custom to go out hunting, with the breeding season over. Khanu set off with some of his men at four a.m. At midday they rested. Kouchow, a shrewd hunter and a good cook, started to skin a stag in the shade of an oak tree. He sliced off the leanest meat and seasoned it with herbs and salt, wrapping it in leaves and straw, and put it in a hole he'd dug. He covered the hole and lit a fire, and left the meat to cook.

Delicious! Said Khanu: 'This I always prefer to home-made.' His men agreed. When they had finished eating they drank tea and lay down to rest in the shade. They talked about whatever Khanu or the elders wanted to.

'There is always something majestic about the mountains. They make one feel so small. In comparison to us, they are enormous and eternal. We are here but a short time. Then we fade into history.'

Jozow started singing a Hayran song (a traditional song of epic poetry). It made his mind drift back to flood-filled nights of battle, when he remembered the cries of the wounded, the clash of swords, and the grinding of shields.

On their way home, the discussion turned to different ways of hunting, what were the best dogs, and the cleverness of greyhounds, quick to find a short cut in chasing down their prey.

'I have been brought up with hunting. A hunter knows his skills, but he should also know how to train his dogs. Best dogs have a strong sense of smell.'

One of the young men interrupted. 'Uncle Kachuow, that is why you hunted that old stag,' he said with a sarcastic smile.

65

Kachuow felt so embarrassed, especially in Khanu's presence. He was so annoyed he turned pale, though didn't reply or face it down. He was staring directly at the mountain path, and had it not been for Khanu's presence would have drawn his sword.

Khanu sensed his disgust, knowing Kachuow to be very touchy. 'No, no, that is not quite right at all. Kachuow's prey is always very good, especially this one. Its antlers we will hang it on the divan's facade, as they're so beautiful.' Khanu looked at him. Kachuow looked back, with a smile of admiration.

A few more added to Kachuow's praises. Then suddenly there was a gentle breeze, as if the trees were holding hands for a Kurdish dance and folk music.

They reached the castle, where all talk was of this year's harvest, of the work done, and of the work not yet finished. Above all the noise was the trampling of horses' hooves, from Hamza's daily training sessions. Khanu turned uphill to see what the regiment was doing.

A huge crowd gathered down below. It was a fine day, the sun was high and bright, and a breeze was whispering in the wood. A group of young men was watching Hamza and his warriors, some of whom Khanu questioned as to these training sessions.

They all seemed impressed with Hamza and his techniques, and remarked on the numbers now joining him. The warriors were in armoured uniform for fencing exercise. Hamza stood to the front of his cadets. 'Get ready! Launch, attack, stop! You shouldn't position your spear like that. You're in a fight, not driving a bull to market.' He showed how it should be done.

He offered advice on the tactics of fighting, most importantly on how to overcome your enemy even when surrounded. Next in line were the archers, and a shooting exercise, using different locations and a variety of riding postures. After training he ordered all to group together, and to pay attention, as some were not making the progress he expected. One serious problem was in the use of spears.

He demonstrated, getting on his horse and charging for 300 yards. Holding his spear firmly he turned back and stuck it in the ground, still controlling the horse, which he brought to a standstill.

He gave as example the Kurdish leader Shierko, who was Saladin Ayubi's uncle. He once said: 'You hold your spear under one arm as if stuck to the back of your horse, so that you, the horse and the spear are as one piece of armour as you charge at the enemy.' Shierko once killed the King of Antakyia in a face-to-face battle, so it was wise to listen to what he said.

It was nearly an hour since Khanu had been back. He was pleased with Hamza and his training, and he promised to give more horses to the best cavaliers: 'Hamza, you do a good job.'

Hamza came forward. 'Delighted,' he said.

'You shall have any assistance you need.' Khanu

turned to Addi, one of his men, and ordered him to arrange for more horses.

Addi was the stable caretaker. He told the young men to bring their own harnesses. 'The horses may not get used to you otherwise.'

'That is certainly right,' one of them replied. 'I have never had more than a donkey.'

Another youth stepped forward. 'We are warriors now. We promise to defend the country. God protect Amir Khanu.'

Khanu faced his young fighters, with Hamza at his side. 'God's peace and mercy upon you,' Hamza said, a chant the warriors repeated.

Said Khanu: 'You must honour the message of your ancestors and defend your country, and be prepared for the ultimate sacrifice. Shah Abbas and the Ottoman sultans want to subvert us. It's our duty to repulse their aggressions, as we have done many times before. We have to support each other.

The tribes, if we join forces together, will be stronger. The enemy will take notice, and may not even attack.' The young fighters, at the beat of a

69

drum, marched back towards the castle in an orderly line, except for some of the archers, who remained for further practice, with their spears and lances and horsemanship. Everyone was happy.

Chapter Four

The Dervish ceremony

Late summer moved to early autumn. There was an aroma of mellow fruits all over the market, in hues of green, yellow, orange, red. Pomegranates, dried figs, black and white grapes piled in heaps, fresh acacia nuts, tomatoes, courgettes, vine leaves, apples and plums dressed the market stalls in sumptuous array. The villagers brought these goods early in the morning, loaded on mules and donkeys, in sacks and in baskets.

Fresh figs oozed with syrup. The pomegranates burst with juice. Black grapes were sold for making pickle, and sultanas for sherbet juice. People would buy most of these fruits to dry and keep for winter, for resale or consumption. Yellow or red grapes were dried to make raisins. Cheese and butter were also on display, which people were able to buy direct from the farmer or in smaller portions from the kiosk traders.

The day's local news was unexpectedly different. A rumour spread in the castle that there was a group of strangers in the region, ten Persian dervishes, the oldest forty-five and the rest in their early twenties and mid-thirties.

They were performing a religious ceremony, arranged in a half circle, their long hair loose and swinging their heads to the rhythm of a drum and daff. (A daff consisted of a light, circular wooden frame, a yard across, covered with dried sheepskin. It was played with both hands, resting on one palm and tapped with fingers of the other hand.) The ceremony was accompanied by magic, involving swords and long knives, as if the performers were stabbing themselves, though without inflicting serious injury. Every day there were more and more spectators, people amazed by what they saw, and paying good money.

Late one evening, when Khursheed was going

round the castle with his men, he came across the dervish group in front of one of the shops. They looked suspicious, and were furtive when observed. On seeing Khursheed they made to disappear. Khursheed went inside the shop. The master wasn't there, but there was a young man tidying up, cleaning and sweeping.

'Where is your master?' Khursheed asked.

'He went home, sir,' the boy said.

'Have the dervish group come in? What did they want? Did they ask for anything?' Khursheed enquired impatiently.

'They asked about what we were doing here, and how many of us.'

Khursheed's suspicion and anxiety increased, while he had to concede the dervishes' popularity was growing each day. Now they had got to the stage of asking for gifts and money.

People generously gave what they could afford,

even when they couldn't communicate properly, because they couldn't speak Persian.

The next day, Khanu and his men came across the dervish group at the castle cave.

'What are these idiots doing here? We don't want their witchcraft.' Khanu sounded angry.

His men were surprised too, as was his son Sifudeen, who was head of the castle guards. Khanu asked him what he knew.

'They haven't been here,' he said. 'Our guards pay no attention to them. I do. According to the laws of Islam, a dervish can go anywhere he wants, but I'm not having that. I dismissed them.'

Khanu's suspicions were aroused, and he sent for Khursheed before he and his men entered the cave. The master came to greet them. 'I am very glad to see you.'

'How is your work?' Khanu enquired.

'God protect you,' the master replied.

'We are the masters of northern Mesopotamia,'

Khanu said with a smile. 'You know who built this castle?'

'Yes sir, I know him. I have heard about him. He was from Erzroum. He built a castle similar to yours in Mardeen.'

Khanu was pleased and impressed with his work. He was making swords, daggers, spears, lances and gunpowder boxes, from materials brought from Tabriz and Erzroum.

'When are you going to put these new pieces together? I would like to test them myself.'

'Next Friday, sir, after midday prayer.'

Khanu, still anxious, left the cave. He called to Khursheed. 'I wanted to talk to you about these dervishes. Keep an eye on them. I hear they wander around asking questions. That's suspicious.'

'There is nothing for them here.'

'It's obvious and we all know, Shah Abbas has his spies.'

'Yes, I saw them myself near the blacksmith's,'

Khursheed confirmed.

'Why didn't you tell me? Khanu was angry.

'I've been watching them ever since. I was going to arrest them.'

'You must go and arrest them now, and don't stint on the interrogations. Punish them if necessary. Get everything you can out of them. Hurry, before they escape!'

Khursheed started promptly, and not finding them in the market went to tell his guards not to let them out. He summoned more men as soon as he could. News spread rapidly in the castle and in the villages, and soon everyone was on the lookout. It was said they did witchcraft for the sake of money, while others were convinced these dervishes were thieves or spies.

As the hunt progressed, Khursheed came across the castle vet, Khalil, who seemed to know enough that would lead to their arrest.

'They are in the food shop, in Musa's food court.

They bought a lamb and Musa was grilling it for them. They're busy making kebabs. They have made so much money with their witchcraft.'

Soon Khursheed was on their tail, relieved to know they hadn't yet left. He and his men headed for Musa's.

'Let's go, before they finish the lamb.' Khursheed spurred his horse and galloped away, his men following. Musa rushed out. 'Marhaba Khursheed, you are very welcome, please.' The gang of dervishes paid them no attention.

Musa showed his new guests to a corner of the shop. 'Please, over there, Khursheed.'

'Thank you, Ali, but you see I'm in a hurry.' He turned to the dervishes, and in Persian asked if they'd finished their meal. They didn't seem to understand, or pretended they didn't. They got up as if to leave.

Khursheed ordered his men to arrest them, and take their belongings: the drums, wind pipe, daffs, everything. 'Search them thoroughly! Tie their arms and take them to the castle.'

The dervishes didn't try to resist, as if they'd expected this all along. They knew they couldn't escape, or wouldn't get far.

Khursheed sent more men to where they'd been staying, with instructions to bring everything from there to castle headquarters.

The gang was detained for nearly a month, and said nothing.

'They admit no guilt, sir,' Khursheed reported to Khanu. 'They answer no questions.'

'Tomorrow afternoon we will have a meeting, the tribe leaders and the castle veterans. We will discuss it then. Bring the dervishes to the divan.'

Nothing could be justified without a confession. And anyway, some religious leaders doubted their guilt, as the dervishes wouldn't betray God. They were self-disciplined, very devout Muslims. Nevertheless, they brought before Khanu and his council of elders.

'Undo their hands. Come forward.' Khanu asked the dervish leader to perform a ceremony, but he protested.

'They have taken our musical instruments.'

A daff was brought to him. He played. It started:

'Hei, hei, hei, Allah!' Then a short pause. Then again, 'Hei, hei, hei, Allah, hei, hei. Hei, Allah.' The performance seemed to be better than at any time before, when the dervishes were free. Khanu turned to one of his associates.

'They think, with swinging their heads and uttering holy words, they can get away with it.'

The dervishes clasped hands in a ring, the leader in the middle, then suddenly broke off in a dance and were turning round and spinning individually, then in two lines facing each other.

'Hei, Allah. Hei, hei, hei, Allah, hei, hei.' At intervals the leader stopped with a shout. 'Hei, hei, hei,' the rest would say, 'hei, Allah.'

He brought them to a standstill. They pushed their heads back and raised their chins with closed eyes and paused for a few seconds, then suddenly, with the elder's voice leading: 'Hei, Allah, hei, hei.'

'Stop it! We have had enough!' Khanu shouted.
The assembly went quiet, watching and listening.
Khanu laid into the dervishes: 'Tell us the truth!
Why are you here? Who sent you?'

They were silent, apart from the elder. 'We are
dervishes, sir. Our duty is to pray to God. We are
allowed, according to Islam, to travel the length and
breadth of the world. It is our duty to do our
ceremony and stay faithful to God. Believe us, sir,
nobody has sent us.'

Khursheed came forward: 'If you are true
believers in God, what were you doing at the local
manufacturers, in front of the cave, and at the
blacksmith's shop?'

The veterans were whispering to one another,
their earlier sympathy turning to suspicion. 'No more
questions are needed. Hang them, hang them.'

The dervishes started their ceremony again, as a
cover-up for their own anxiety.

'Stop that! I say it's enough,' shouted Khanu.' He turned to the assembly 'It's quite obvious now they are spies. They can't get away with stories and lies. We have been through this before with magicians and witches. We will make you confess.'

He ordered the guards to bring forward Mullah Kadir, as an example, who had gone through a similar experience. He was asked to tell the story of his confession, when he was pardoned and let off. Mullah was tall and bony, an aged man with soft feeble eyes, wrinkled, and wearing a white turban.

'There were times when Shah Abbas sent in spies, each time with a different pretext: as a merchant, a sophist, a dervish, a beggar, and so on. Plan was to obtain military secrets and castle plans, and statistics regarding men, weapons and ammunition. The spies were promised gold. Such temptation overpowered their religious belief, and dented their honesty. But as you see, they were not always successful.'

An old man stood. 'God will protect our leader, Khanu. Whoever tries to destroy us, or insult our dignity and well being, must be punished. Do these people have no fear of God? They spy for our enemies, against our castle, and our villages. Do we now watch them slaughter our children? What are we waiting for? They must be executed!'

For this there was general agreement. 'Yes! Yes! They should be hanged. God is just.'

The ultimate decision rested with Khanu. He ordered his men to tie their hands and put them in a cell. 'I will announce their punishment in due course.'

The youngest dervish cried out. 'Release my hands, I will tell you the truth. I will tell you everything.' Khanu had him separated from the rest, and listened to what he had to say.

'It is now two years since my parents left me with this group of dervishes. Being poor, they couldn't feed me. We are a group of 300. Our leader is an old sheikh. We have to keep most of what we get for him, and in return he gives us a little.

We have with us people from Afghanistan, Azerbaijan, Persia and Kurdistan. We were sent by the governor of Tebriz. When I heard about the castle, I wanted to come here. We have been told to find out as much as we can, to lay hands on whatever information there is, and pass it on to the king's men.'

Khanu had the young man released and let off. He was separated from the rest, but not allowed to leave the castle.

Later, an announcement was made in the market and at the mosque, concerning a group of nine dervishes, who were due to be hanged, on the following Thursday, at dawn, after morning prayer. They had been shown to be spies of Shah Abbas.

Anyone could come and witness the execution. It was a just punishment, for conspiracy and betrayal, for the dishonesty of a group of dervishes who acted in the name of God.

83

Chapter Five

The wedding

Isfahan, the capital of the Safavid Empire, was its most delightful setting, for its mosques – Masjid-i Jami, Masjid-i Shah and Lutf-ullah – and the garden of Chihil Sutun Palace. With its forty pillars, that had one of the most elaborate of the world's architectures.

It was built by Shah Abbas when he moved the capital from Casvin to Isfahan in 1608. The most prominent feature of all was Chahar Bagh, the 'four gardens'.

It was like a Persian garden carpet, but conjured into three dimensions, opulent with flowers, streams, trees and fountains, astonishing to all who visited.

It was said that no contemporary city in the world could rival Isfahan. Chahar Bagh was a huge venue, some four kilometres from its north to its south axis. It encompassed the royal garden bordering the Maidan and the Hazar Jarib, a royal estate south of

Zayandarud. Stately plane trees planted in rows divided three alleys, the central one of which contained a canal and fountains. Gardens spread far and wide on either side. Trellised, rather than solid walls, allowed passers-by to glimpse from the public thoroughfares. There were, at intervals, palaces with names like Satars, Abasabad, Jahan Nama and Nastaran. Long vistas flanked by palaces were enclosed at either end by monumental buildings.

Forming a natural pendant to the Chahar Bagh and to Julfa was a bridge that linked these two projects. It was founded by Shah's favourite general, Allahvardi Khan, and named after him, a remarkable 300 metres garnished with pavilions. One prominent building was the portal of the tomb of Harun-I Vilayat, 'the patron', the grand vizier Durmish Khan, who is mentioned in a Persian distichal inscription: 'In whose honour it was built'. The exterior elevation of the dome illustrated in miniature the piecemeal nature of the whole. Its octagonal base gave way to a square middle storey.

86

The dome rested on a high cylindrical drum set over a modest octagon, and had a slight bulge at the collar; the façade subtly exploited the plastic potential of the arched niche, which repeated at various scales and depths its leitmotiv on the entire composition. It was ornamented with lapidary in dusky gold lettering, which stood out from the white used elsewhere.

The Maidan (the main square) was fronted with a low two-storey arcade, which defined its limits and made it a piazza rather than a sprawling field. Shops on the ground floor opened to dwellings above, but their lowness had a further aesthetic impact – it exalted the stature of the four buildings that broke through the arcade.

The Maidan was lined with 'chinnar' cypress trees and a water channel, while no building intruded on its open space, which played a vital part in the life of the city.

By turns it was a marketplace, a training and parade ground, an execution dock, a polo pitch, a running track, and an arena for animal combat. It was a magnificently illustrated funfair by night, and the inevitable setting for all kinds of royal entertainment.

Monumental portals at the centre of each short side gave access to the Masjid-I Shah and the Qaissary. Ali Capu and Qaissary portals bore the symbol of Sagittarius.

These buildings were decorated with carvings from the Khusraw and Shirin romantic epic, with a fresco showing lovers in a landscape, painted in a niche with clouds in the margins in pale blue and gold.

There were paintings by Agha Riza, Mani, Behzad and Sadiqi Beg. Of the standing figures one was of a girl holding a fan, another of an elegant youth holding a fruit bowl – this bore the signature of Agha Riza. There were line drawings of a young girl standing and holding a rosary, and a seated youth with a spray of flowers, signed Ali Qapu Pavilion Isfahan. [See *The Cambridge History of Iran*, vol 6, pp761, 763, 777, Cambridge University Press. 1985.]

In autumn, when the summer heat had cooled, the green leaves began to change colour. It was in quieter season that the king was getting married. The bride was the daughter of the Afghan king. The main festivities were in the king's Chahar Bagh garden.

Its roses and shrubs reflected in the ponds and pools, which were thronged with domestic and wild birds. The canals were edged and ornamented with marble lined with bronze, with wooden benches bankside. Guests the king had invited were staying at the palace in the western quarter of the garden, and included kings, ministers, merchants, deputies and tribal leaders. Some of these were Kurdish leaders, close allies of Shah Abbas. Parties and festivities were not only at the palace, but in other quarters in Isfahan.

The main Isfahan square, 'the Maidan', was packed. A marquee had been set up for the king in the palace garden, for his occasional visits. Benches, seats and rich carpeting had been laid out, arranged according to rank.

The procession started in the afternoon: 300

horses led in golden trappings. On foot were 450 ghulams (young boys) with javelins in their hands. Next to them were 300 warriors in brocade with armour beneath, and carrying swords. Behind them were 700 falconers with sparrow hawks.

After the falconers were 300 men on horseback. There were also seventy lions and leopards chained together firmly, in coats of Chinese brocade. These were all trained and muzzled with gold chains.

Accompanying all were 2,000 minstrels playing airs, each mounted on a camel, wearing embroidered royal overcoats with red and gold stripes, and with golden coronets on their heads.

There were chairs, benches and large pavilions as well as small canvas shelters for the men and women. There also came 200 captains of war with kindle braziers, in which were burned incense and ambergris. There were 200 young attendant girls carrying roses and perfumes before the Shah.

Escorting the king himself were thirty princes on

horseback, all clad in coats of yellow, red and violet. There were 150 warriors to the front, with the rest to the rear. The king's black cart was embroidered with gold, jewels and ornaments of precious stone.

The king sat arrayed in his crown, royal coat, bracelets, collar and golden girdle. Every button in it was set with jewels. A grand vizier accompanied him, with two guards with spears and swords standing on each side of the cart. Black horses pulled the cart, their red leather strapping ornamented with gold.

The bride, Pervin Khanum, was sitting on the royal bench surrounded by maids and servants. She was being told of cavalcade approaching with the king at its head.

She donned a dress scented with musk, while her face had a rosy tint. On her chest was red Grecian brocade. Her whole frame was a mass of jewels on a background of gold. On her head was placed a royal diadem wholly composed of Pahlavi jewels.

She could not hold back tears of happiness, which rolled down her cheeks. With the king's arrival she rose to her feet, showing her full stature, and greeted him. Both sat to watch and enjoy the wedding celebrations.

By early evening every corner was lit with candles and chandeliers, and magicians, comedians, song, music and dance cheered the wedding. Extracts from Shah Nama were recited, with the romance of Khosraw, Perviz and Shirin, Rostam and Zal, and with the story of Bahman son of Asfandiyar. [See *The Epic of the Kings*, by Shah Nama, translated by Ruben Levy, published 1967, Routeledge & Kegan Paul Ltd.]

The king's family and relatives, especially the ladies, had their own quarters and a schedule of celebration. Faiza Khanim, one of the king's wives, and her daughter-in-law Zuleikha, were sitting at the head of the guests, watching groups of women musicians and dancers taking their turn. One of the festivity's great surprises saw two huge elephants with men on their backs driven into the midst of things. It was said that the Indian king had offered them to Shah Abbas, with the elephants trained especially for the occasion. They took glasses of drink in their trunks, without spillage, and placed them on the tables before the guests.

The celebration went on smoothly, though no one was aware of what else was on the king's mind. His main worry was Dum Dum Castle, which had blocked his way into Kurdistan, had refused to pay taxes, and hadn't offered any army recruits.

The king was anxious for news, having great hope for his spies, the dervishes, who were due to report back soon. Did he seem to foresee their fate? He retired with celebrations in full swing, and left it to his grand vizier to make his apologies. 'His Majesty needs rest.' With the king more uneasy than ever regarding the dervishes, he sent for his head of military, who had similar inklings that the news wasn't good. In fact the king was now so angry he gave orders for an immediate attack on the castle, under the leadership of Sulaiman Khan. The idea was to destroy the castle and capture Khanu and bring him before the king.

One of his ministers suggested delaying until spring, as the coming winter would make battle more difficult, and heavy snow sometimes rendered the mountains impassable. The king didn't like that idea. 'This is my final order. There can be no delay. Proceed immediately!' No one dared utter a word in defiance.

'Your Majesty's order is applied herewith. The army will be ready.'

Later, when the king returned to his guests, he thought it over and saw the sense of his minister's suggestion. This was not the right time to launch an attack. In the morning he sent for Sulaiman Khan.

Khan arrived at the palace, apprehensive. He bowed and kneeled to his king.

'Sulaiman, don't take too many men – 100 or 150 ought to be enough. Reconnoitre the castle. Observe what Khanu has done, with his military preparations, with his weapons, enforcement and so on. What does he want to do? Find out if he's willing to pay taxes, and how loyal he is to the empire.'

Khan bowed and stepped back to the door. 'Your majesty, as soon as it is possible.'

Sulaiman Khan decided on a Kurdish tribal leader as guide, giving him the uniform of an Iranian combatant, not someone to be recognised around the castle. His name was Bakir Beig, and he cautioned against the cold and unpredictable weather of the mountains of Kurdistan. He spoke also of the Bradoust tribe – a big tribe – one occupying not only the castle, but a vast area surrounding.

Soon, Sulaiman Khan and his men were on their way to the castle. When they reached the foot of the mountains, Khan took Bakir Beig aside. 'You are a man of the mountains. In Asfahan you predicted snowfall. You know the moods and climate of your country.'

'Yes, we predict the changes. We live with it from our childhood. We read the sun and moon, and the behaviour of birds, and of other animals.'

When they were closer to the castle, snowfall was even heavier. It came in icy flurries, with dark clouds massed over the mountains. The guards huddled together with their heavy woollen cloaks drawn tightly around them. The days were bleak, and the advancing army found its progress impeded, slipping on the glassy rocks. They stumbled down the valleys, through snowbound villages, then out onto a blank white landscape.

Khanu was informed by his villagers of the arrival of Sulaiman Khan and his men. As Khanu didn't want them too close to the castle, he went out to them. They met in the village of Razaw. With such foul weather, Khanu wondered how the Persian convoy managed to find its way here. Bakir Beig reassured Sulaiman Khan that with God's mercy they would find their way back. Said Khanu: 'We have a hard life. You see how rugged are the mountains. There is little land to cultivate. It is hard to make a living. But as God is our witness, we do not intend harm to anyone. What does His Majesty want from us? Tell him we are peace-loving people, who possess little of value to pay him dues.'

After a few days' talk and rest the weather changed. Khan and his men made their way back, as the grip of the severe weather eased. When they reached Bride Spring a few of his men saw a stag at the brook, and gave chase. The stag leapt and ran uphill to a snow-covered mountain, causing an avalanche. It left all in its wake with little chance of escape. About thirty men were buried under the snow, though Sulaiman Khan and Bakir Beig escaped unhurt, being far behind the convoy. They made their way into the valleys and the villages there.

Bride Spring was the name derived from a tragic story. It told of a convoy passing near the spring, and of a bride bound for another village. They were caught similarly in an avalanche, with the whole wedding party buried under the snow. Their bodies weren't recovered until the spring, when the weather brought a thaw.

After four months, the bodies were as fresh as the day the avalanche had struck. The story tells of the bridegroom's relatives anxiously awaiting their arrival, but finally sending out a search party. Its members, when they reached Bride Spring, found the valley almost filled with snow, but it was unclear if anyone had been lost to the avalanche. They still had hope, but searched to no avail. That is how the name was applied – Bride Spring. The relatives accepted the decrees of destiny, that it was God's will, therefore the bodies were buried there. It was believed that victims of natural disasters all went to heaven. Ever since, Bride Spring had been a sacred place, with passers-by whispering prayers and showing respect.

On the evening when Sulaiman Khan reached Asfahan, one of the palace servants told His Majesty of their return. Sulaiman Khan went before his king and paid his respects, bowing and kneeling.

'Talk! Tell us what happened!'

'God protect Your Majesty. There were still two days for us to reach the castle. Khanu came to greet us. I would rather have carried on to the castle myself, but the weather made it impossible.' He went on to talk of the avalanche.

The king asked about Khanu.

'Your Majesty, Khanu protests he has nothing to spare. There is not enough land for them to cultivate. Their survival hangs by a thread. We should wait for the right time, then deal with him.'

'I must demolish his castle!' the king insisted. Would the season aid his ambition?

In winter, when the mountains of Kurdistan were covered with snow, the villagers were idle, apart from occasionally hunting wild animals. They lived off their rations, prudently stocked in summer: dried vegetables, cooked sheep, goat and lamb preserved in animal fat, dried figs and plums pressed tightly into goat skins, and a variety of nuts, grain and dried fruit.

Winter was the season of relaxation, a time for friends and relatives to visit each other, and play games or read stories and poetry. A traditional game involved scarves and woollen socks. Two people or more decide on a number of turns. Marks are gained from winning when turns are taken hiding a silver coin or a ring. The hiding place is under one of five different piles of these scarves and socks. Guesses are made as to which one. Initially the game would start with a bet. The loser would have to buy something for the winner, such as a chicken. These were simple pleasures, and the cause of much merriment and laughter.

Chapter Six

In summer the sheep stayed in the mountains for long periods, and quite often a family member would go up, well stocked with provisions, to help the shepherd. The Maqsood family, who had a big herd, often sent their daughter Dilbar and her little brother. Dilbar would take a horse, and a mule loaded with necessaries – honey, bread, butter. Her little brother would sit atop the loaded mule and she would ride the horse.

'My dear daughter, be careful with milking the herd. The lambs need milk, and leave some for the shepherd.' When sheep gave birth, it was important not to drain their milk to the last drop, as their lambs were in need of nutrition, to fight off the cold and possible disease. Her mother was emphatic about that.

'Mum, do you think I'm still a child? It's as if I've never been in the mountains, or do you take me for an idiot?' Dilbar was annoyed with her mother.

'I like just to remind you. I'm sure you can manage.' She kissed her little son. 'Take care, my castle cavalier. You're going to tell me all about it when you're back. You'll love it up there. Now go, and God protect you.'

It was early evening, and it took them two hours to reach the herd. The shepherd greeted them warmly, as he knew he was in for some homemade bread and other delicacies. He would tell them all about the new lambs that had been born the day before.

Every day about five or six sheep gave birth, so the size of the herd was gradually increasing. As usual, the shepherd would start to tease Dilbar.

101

'Look, you're a grown woman now, so your mum doesn't come. She sends you instead.'

'Our neighbours say my presence graces anywhere I go,' Dilbar said jokingly, with a smile. Soon other shepherds came to visit, especially now there was a newcomer.

Dilbar said to them, 'Listen, brothers, I know you have been out here for a long time. If anyone needs help preparing food, just let me know. I'd love to cook for all of you.'

The elder shepherd came forward. 'At first I was disappointed, as your mother didn't come, but now you are here in her place, may God protect you, little angel.'

She woke early in the morning, and started milking the herd. She put aside the shepherds' share of milk and some to make yoghurt. The shepherds were all so pleased with her presence, and everyone would tease and joke with her. 'Who is the lucky man who will have you as a wife?'

'Yes, who?' she'd reply. 'Perhaps one of these

young shepherds.' But most of the young shepherds knew about her lover, and would whisper, 'She belongs to Addi's son.'

When the elder shepherd heard that he raised his voice. 'God will protect both of you, my dear. He is an honourable gentleman. You are such a match for each other. I wish you the best. God will rain his grace on you.'

She covered her face with her hands and turned away. She was a bit shy in the face of this kind of talk.

Khursheed, the market inspector, soon learned of Dilbar's whereabouts, and became restless, desperate to see her, especially when he had plenty of time on his hands. One day he got ready with his wife to go to the mountains, and left his castle duties to one of his assistants.

He left his wife with his herd some distance away from where Dilbar was situated, and went off to find her. He thought over his plan and wondered what to say when he met her, and what she would do. He was

103

going to pretend that the lambs in his herd were dying, and was here to seek Khasraw's, the elder shepherd's, advice. Khasraw knew a lot about livestock and their diseases.

Khursheed, when he discovered where Dilbar was, went to her tent, which high up in the mountain was ornamented with coloured loops and beads of wool and stones. She wasn't there, as she'd gone to fetch water from the spring in the valley. Her younger brother greeted him. On her way back from the spring, laden with her goatskin calabash, Dilbar saw the horse in front of her tent and wondered whose it was. 'I hope nothing bad has happened at home.' She was anxious.

'God forbid, what has happened? Who is it?' she shouted. She didn't recognise the horse. When she put down the water and went inside she was disgusted to see who it was.

'Welcome back, my beauty,' Khursheed said.

She didn't answer.

'I have come to see your shepherd. A strange

disease has struck my herd, especially the lambs. I need his advice.' Khursheed explained.

'Go to him then. Why come here? May none of your lambs survive. Don't you know at midday no shepherd is at home?' She knew he was telling lies, and what his true intentions were. Khursheed was really annoyed, especially at his own folly.

'Dilbar, Dilbar my love! You have been unfair. I love you so much. Where will you find a husband like me? I will shower you with gold, silver and jewels – jewels from Baghdad, jewels from Asfahan.'

Dilbar grew even angrier. 'You are a savage. If you had any integrity, you wouldn't come at an hour when I'm by myself. How many times do I have to tell you? There is no point pursuing me. You are married, and too old for me. Anyway I don't fancy you! What's more my parents don't like you! Aren't you ashamed? A true gentleman once refused doesn't return – not if he has any pride.' She was pale with anger. 'I have refused you so many times, and still you come. If you don't stop, I will tell my brothers to tear you to pieces! This is my final warning. You cannot force me to marry you. Besides, I have someone else.'

'You'll regret this,' Khursheed said with a frown.

Dilbar left the tent and whispered to her brother, 'Go and release his horse and scare it away.'

When at length Khursheed followed her out, his horse had disappeared.

'What! Where is it? It can't have been stolen!' He couldn't believe what he saw.

'You can't even look after your own horse and you want to get married again,' Dilbar said with a sarcastic smile. He searched everywhere, and couldn't find it – it was nowhere to be seen. He rushed down the slope.

The shepherds looked after him and shouted to each other. 'Look! Look! His horse has deserted him. How the market traders *will* be relieved.' They were all laughing.

As the morning wore on, the sun grew more intense and the breeze faded. Dilbar walked down to the stream, a tall, slender figure, filled with grace and confidence. She stepped from the stream and sat down to think.

Nanie saw her from her tent, and came down to meet her. Dilbar told her of Khursheed, of his talk of gold and jewels, and of how she had sent her brother to shoo away his horse. They had a good laugh. 'He has been turned down so many times, but he doesn't give up.'

'He is madly in love with you, but you don't have to be so cruel.' They both giggled.

'He has five children. His oldest son is older than my brother. He's to finish his religious studies with Mullah Rasheed, then he will have military training with Hamza. Khursheed should find *him* a wife, and not be looking for one for himself.' Dilbar dipped her hand in the stream. 'He thinks that as castle inspector he has an important position. *My* favourite is a brave cavalier.'

The sky lit up with the orange glow of evening, and from where they sat the fields were covered with purple, red and yellow flowers. Most of their coevals were still out in the mountains, fields and orchards, bowed under backbreaking labour, women and children not exempt, as now there was a harvest to gather. But it was a time not only of work, but of celebration too, with picnics in the offing, especially for the young. And such a socialising atmosphere.

There was no sense of individual material possession, as everyone lived as a large family. Shepherds joked. The young teased them in return, stealing their hats. 'If you can't protect your hat, what chance your herds?'

The year before, there was an attack on the castle, leaving a small number dead and wounded, and a period of mourning. The herds, in an unusually prolific season, had cheered them slightly, as that was the main source of income and livelihood.

In light of Khursheed's visit, Nanie, Shabab's sister, urgently sent for her brother. The family wondered what had happened. When they asked Gadeu, the messenger, he assured them it was nothing serious. That evening Shabab jumped on his horse and left for the mountains, despite his mother urging him not to go until morning. He didn't listen.

He was worried by what he had heard, and took his armour. It was after midnight when he arrived. The dogs gathered barking round him, but he knew their names and settled them down. Meanwhile, in all the commotion, the shepherds had gone for their weapons, relaxing only when they saw it was Shabab.

'It's only me,' he shouted. 'Anything wrong?'

'Only that we're surprised to see you.'

'Does anyone know why my sister sent for me?'

'God forbid, no, sir. As far as we know there's nothing to worry about.'

The trees, tents, shrubs, horses and the mountain slopes were bathed in a silvery glow of moonlight. Shabab went to his sister's tent. He found her asleep. Her long lashes were gently closed together under the tiny curve of her eyebrows. Her full lips were like a flower bud. She was breathing softly. Her long plaits were strewn on her feather pillow. A thin woollen blanket covered her. He crept in quietly, lowered his head, and whispered her name. 'Nanie, Nanie.'

She woke up alarmed, but soon recognised him. 'My dear brother, I never thought— You are here so fast. On the wind's wing.'

'You sent for me urgently. Father and mother are worried. What has happened? The shepherds say there is nothing.'

'That is right. It's not serious. Let me get up. I will talk to you.'

Shabab went out and looked at the newly born lambs. They were like human infants when asleep, contentedly hugging each other. Some of the bigger ones were chewing, or cudding, in their sleep. They bleated when he approached. One of the shepherds spoke. 'They fare very well. Look at those newborns.' He picked out his favourite, which he'd kept for himself.

'They fare well indeed,' said Shabab. 'You are masters of your trade.' With that he returned to his sister's tent. She had put her bed away and rolled out a woollen rag. She had fresh milk put aside for morning tea, though the yoghurt wasn't yet ready. She called everyone to breakfast. Shabab was wondering why he'd been sent for.

She knew he was worried, 'My dear brother, fear not. As soon as the shepherds have had their breakfast, I will talk.' She showed him the bread she'd made. 'There is fresh cheese and honey too.'

The shepherds attended to the lambs, whose mothers gave suckle, before they had their breakfast. After they had left, Nanie told the story of Khursheed's recent visit. 'He still presses Dilbar to marry him, and boasts about his wealth.'

'Then he's pressed his suit once too often,' said Shabab. 'You wait till I find him.'

His sister pleaded, trying to reassure him that Dilbar never would give in. Just then, up on the hill, a shepherd with flute was singing a pastoral song, appropriate to the situation.

'Coned with a sieve, coned with a sieve,
As if you are coned with a sieve.
Your lamb has been stolen.
Your lamb has been stolen.
Now you are so restless,

Do you think you have been deceived?'

The lyric seemed to bespeak Dilbar's contention
with Khursheed.

Shabab, when his horse had grazed, saddled up
and went in search of his rival. It was midday when
he neared Khursheed's tent. Across the brook
children were playing, jumping in the water, or
sword fighting with sticks, or climbing in the trees.
He pulled up. 'Anyone know Khursheed's tent?'

A little girl came forward. ' Uncle Shabab,
Kursheed's tent is over there.' She pointed. 'By those
trees, second on the left.' In front of it was a plump
middle-aged woman, waiting as if to greet him.

'Brother, what are you waiting for? Come in,
come in. Break bread with us.'

'God rain His grace on your household, but I am
in a hurry. Where is Khursheed?'

'My husband is not here. He is on his way back to
the castle. He has lost his horse.'

'How so?' Shabab enquired.

'He was away, but I don't know. He tells me

little.'

Shabab, who knew about the horse, turned back towards the castle. Once there, his father greeted him.

'You come at the right moment. Khanu has asked us into the divan. There is a meeting.'

Shabab had a quick wash, devoured his dinner hastily, and went to the meeting. He knew he shouldn't raise the issue of Khursheed, but rather wait to see what he did.

The divan was so crowded there was hardly space to sit. The atmosphere seemed very weighty. With the guests so many, a steward suggested that a group of young men could be moved to the garden, and a few carpets with pillows and mattresses were taken out. When Khanu arrived the congregation rose. He urged them back down. All fell silent, but Khanu was in no hurry.

He appeared to be waiting for someone. An old veteran with full battle gear arrived. He might have been eighty-five or more, though looked fit and steady. By the looks he was one of Khanu's relations, similarly built, slimmer perhaps, with soft hazel eyes, bushy eyebrows, and a thick white beard framing his sunken mouth. Khanu stood in respect, and the rest followed. He moved towards Khanu and turned to the guests:

'I was young once. I was in charge of Mansur Beg's herd. It numbered 400 – more. There were twenty stallions. Ten horses. One horse was a three-year-old – my favourite. I trained him. I shared my bread and sweet with him. Whenever I played the pipe, he came to me. He stood with me. One day I ran out of bread. I went without for two days. There was no one else – I couldn't leave the herd. At last on the third day I left the herd and got bread. When I got back, the herd had gone. I searched for days. I found – nothing. I thought Azeri, or Persian bandits, must have taken them. That was what they did.'

The old vet paused for a sip of water, and glanced at the gathering. 'I got my chance, killing two of those who had robbed me. I left them to rot. They

were eaten by vultures. When I told Mansur Beg
what had happened, he was angry. He threatened to
skin my head and stuff it with straw, if I didn't find
the herd. He vowed to visit his rage on my family.

I looked for days, but in vain. I just couldn't find
them.' He stopped to raise his turban and scratch his
head. The assembly listened, silent. 'I looked far and
wide. I couldn't find them. Tired, I almost gave up,
when on a high mountain. I fell asleep. I dreamt of
the herd. I was with them, playing my flute. I
suddenly woke with joy. I had remembered the tune I
played on my flute. Had remembered the melody for
my favourite horse.'

He paused to wipe his eyes. 'I played the melody.
It seemed its sound echoed in the mountains, in the
valleys. I stopped. "Is it a dream?" I thought. I heard
the neighing of a horse, as if still in a dream. It was
all so unlikely. I played again. The neighing got
nearer, but I couldn't see anything. I was happy, and
started to laugh out loud. I played over and over, and
heard my horse's hooves, but still couldn't see him.
Then I did see him, my white horse, and all the rest

115

of the herd, following.' He choked with emotion.

'He, leading the herd, when he got nearer, and
saw me, stood perfectly still, his ears erect. He
stared, as if about to speak, impossibly. "Here we
are, at last we have found each other." Now again he
was pleased to share my bread, which I pulled from
my trunk. I stroked his neck and patted his forehead,
and rode him again. Without delay, I took the herd
back to the village. My problem was over. Mansur
Beg urged me to break bread with him, but I didn't
accept. He tried to keep me working for him, but I no
longer wished to. I had had enough.'

His story, he knew, sounded naïve, innocent, but
he still held their attention. 'Mansur Beg was harsh
not only with me. His tribe were fed up. When he
died, they showed their relief.'

What this old tribal vet had meant by his tale was
not to give up. You had to work hard to defend your
people, and stay loyal to your leader. The next
speaker *was* their leader, Khanu.

'Can you all see now why I have called you here?' An old man stood up. 'No, sir, nobody knows.'

Khanu put them right. 'We know that the Shamdinan tribe is under continual attack by the Turkish Army, for refusing to pay taxes. We are trying to get more information. It's not clear how the Shamdinans are coping. If they need it, we must send help.'

He turned to the veterans to gauge their reaction, as it was their backing he needed. With no hesitation, all showed their readiness to help. 'God protect you, sir,' said one old man. 'With God's will, this is the most courageous undertaking. We are at your service.'

'Yes, as God is our witness, we are ready for the fight,' others added.

It was agreed to help the Shamdinans. Khanu started to draw up a plan, with the tribal leaders backing him. 'My father,' Khanu said, 'was in the thick of it the last time they were attacked. No one but us went to their assistance. We all know, since

117

the castle was built, the Persians and Ottomans have longed to destroy it and subjugate us all. With the help of merciful God, we will defend our country, as always. But we have to be on our guard and ready to fight.'

Now even more expressed their support. 'God protect you, sir. God protect you and us. We will fight for the honour of our homeland.'

Threats of attack on the Kurds had become a way of life, and it was to no one's surprise when there was news of enemy activity. Only the year before, the castle militia had been to help the Shikak tribe against the Turks. The Shamdinan region was closer, on the other side of the Turkish border, and more vulnerable to Ottoman attack, as neither the Ottoman Turks nor the Persians had absolute control over it.

Chapter Seven

The Emir of Shamdinan, Mir Sadiq, was in his divan with his tribal heads and religious leaders. They had gathered to discuss the situation and arrive at a plan to repulse the Turks.

They knew about the capacity of the Turkish Army. They knew that the purpose of the enemy's offensive was to wipe out all resistance. No one wished to pay taxes, especially to both the Persians and the Turks. Qadzi Bieg had been in charge of his men when facing the latter.

It was now his turn to put forward some suggestions. 'Why,' he asked, 'do you think we should ask the help of anyone *but* Khanu? Is there anyone in Kurdistan stronger than him? Khanu is the only hope. The castle's military infrastructure is crucial. Did not he and his people help the Shikaks? Without them, they'd have been crushed by the Ottomans.'

Mir Sadiq was one of the most prominent warrior

119

leaders. He was well known for his shrewdness, wisdom and courage, and had never hesitated in leading the fight against marauding enemies. He was a statesman as well as a battlefield vet, with experience of hunting, farming, cattle, breeding, trade – to name but few. He was literate, with a love of books, and could be relied on to settle local disputes.

Qadzi Bieg took the floor. 'God protect our Emir. To ask Khanu for help must be one of our first options. There is no shame in asking aid of our compatriots, especially Khanu. I am sure he won't let us down. We know that. Two years ago he helped the Tagur tribe. Last year he helped rescue the Shikaks. We should send an envoy to him.'

There was general support for that suggestion.

A few names were mentioned, and they settled on Mir Sadiq's brother and Abdul Razaq, who was a well-known army commander. They were primed to deliver a message to Dum Dum Castle. The letter was prepared by the Emir himself, and was made ready for immediate dispatch, the situation being so desperate. 'Give Khanu my sincere salutation. Tell him our situation is dire. We are on the verge of wipeout by the savage Turk. We all know very well what the Turkish sultans want from us.'

'We will have to take Simon, the merchant. He knows the way and all the short cuts.'

'So be it.' The Emir sent for Simon, stressing the need for the shortest possible route to Dum Dum Castle. Simon was a Jewish trader, who knew the castle well, having been there many times. The next day, at dawn, he and the two messengers set off.

As they neared their goal, twenty-five castle guards spotted them from higher ground, deep in the valley thickets. Four men were assigned, who would ambush and overpower them if they were strangers sent with ill intent. As it turned out, they were ordered to stop and identify themselves.

'Who are you? What is your mission?'

'Salamun alaikum brothers, we are messengers from Shamdinan, sent by Mir Sadiq, Mir of

Shamdinan. We have a message for Khanu.'

The castle guard went down to meet them, to check on their legitimacy. The letter was enough to justify what they said. They were integrated into the group, and informed they were at a day's reach from the castle.

They were invited to a meal of fish from the river, while the horses were watered and grazed. Discussion soon turned to the Turks and their attacks, and how precious was the harvest. After a few hours' rest, they headed towards the castle, breaking their journey at a spring, where they camped for the night. They moved on again at dawn, in a twitter of birdsong, and with the rising sun, and on through the changing hues of morning – its greys, browns and greens flaming into russet, red and yellow. These were those simple spectacular sights that inspired a man to defend his freedom to the last.

One among the guards was so overcome he pointed to the mountain summit, which was just then a corona of golden light, heaven in a nutshell. He was brought back to the reality of the situation when

Simon related his version of how Dum Dum Castle was built.

'I heard it from a man who used to work for me, when I came to the castle often. I brought in materials from Sham (Aleppo). I hired him to guard my caravan. One evening, when we'd finished trading, and put away our loads, this is what he told me.

The castle had been rebuilt when he was very young. The master supervising it was responsible for the building of others before – one for the Persian emperor. There were frequent attacks from the Ottomans, so castles became a necessity. The one he provided for the Safavids was unique. Nothing like it had ever been done before. When the king saw it he was so impressed he sent for the master. When the emperor heard of it, he planned to kill him, so that no new castle could be delivered into enemy hands. The master fled and went into hiding.'

Now they were quite near the castle, but Simon went on with his story.

'The master builder ended up with the Bradoust tribe and started on this enormous castle for Khanu. It was very different from the ones he'd built before. You see, it wasn't *only* a castle. It was a town, a community, with its own government, laws, a judiciary, a militia, and places to live and work. Its inhabitants left the castle only for the purposes of farming and trade. Its three solid walnut doors were set in thick stone walls. There were five towers guarded round the clock. The structure was strong enough to withstand artillery, bombs and stone missiles. There were further towers built in the surrounding mountains, as watch outs.'

With that, someone interrupted: 'You think the castle guard has seen us?'

'Yes, undoubtedly. They'll be waiting to meet us.'

The stones making up the walls were huge and neatly cut, and an amazing feat of engineering. Some were carved with likenesses of warriors, tigers, bears and lions.

By now there were guards outside the castle waiting for them, to inspect and identify them. Simon was recognised by one of them, and they were all taken inside to a guest room. It was floored with huge cobbled stones, and in the foreyard was a pool edged with white marble and flat stones. The pool was filled with water from a stream, which came in under the walls in stone ducts. There was a high ceiling and few windows. The walls were hung with patterned arrases, locally made. The floor was carpeted, and ranged along the walls were cotton mattresses with feather pillows, for guests to relax.

Two young men brought tea, water and yoghurt drink. At a far corner of the room was a bench, from where the guests would be addressed. Weapons hung on the walls: swords, shields, spears, bows, arrows. It was the same with handmade attire: scarves, socks, hats, turbans. Attached to the corners of the ceiling were the skulls of hyenas, lions, tigers, wolves and bears.

Years before, a story went round that a hyena came to eat the sheep and children. It struck several times, till at last someone was assigned to hunt it down. Eventually it was spotted and killed. The hyena's head had hung here ever since.

They were informed that Khanu was on his way to see them. He appeared with his men. In deference, they bowed to kiss his hand. Initially his presence seemed awesome, though when he talked he put them at their ease, so charming and polite a man he was. He wore traditional costume, with a dagger in his belt. They delivered their letter to him.

'I am told you come from Shamdinan,' said Khanu. 'I have been there once, when I was young, before we built the castle. Your country is beautiful. Your people are well, I trust.'

'Yes, great Emir, Shamdinan is a part of heaven, as the locals say. That is why the Turks are tempted. They have tried to conquer us, but with God's will we've repulsed their attacks. This time, they have brought an army to fight us.'

'Yes, I heard about that. We know that the two empires aim to divide our country between them. If they succeed, it will be hard to stop them occupying other parts of Kurdistan.'

Khanu sent for his trusted elders and veterans of war, and briefed them to assist the Shamdinans. Khanu read the letter, whose most moving words were these: 'Our great leader Khanu, we beg your assistance. This time the Turkish Army is big and very strong. We urgently need your help. We beseech you, though our morale is high.' Khanu and his council suggested 600 men, with Hamza Chawesh leading the army. Hamza was honoured to carry out so important a mission against the Turks. Young men cherished the task of defending their country, with Hamza handpicking the best of them – some of the newly trained, and others with experience.

The plan was drawn up: personnel, horses, weapons, rations – all was made ready. Tearful families and friends gathered to say their goodbyes, in the knowledge that some of these soldiers wouldn't return. They were sent off with pipes and drums.

It took a week to reach Shamdinan. Mir Sadiq

greeted their arrival, with intelligence as to the size of the Turkish Army and what he thought it best to do. He was astonished and delighted at the size and organisation of the liberating force. Hamza asked him for thirty Shamdinans to act as guide, as they were not familiar with the territory. They didn't venture too close to the battle zone, and kept hidden in the woodlands.

Hamza rallied his troops. 'We will take rest tonight. Guards are posted. Early tomorrow we launch our attack. I want to see you as tigers and lions. The world must know how Dum Dum Castle fights for the Kurds – with passion and without mercy. God bless you.'

In the night a Turkish soldier was captured and brought for questioning. He turned out to be a Kurd, and was obliging with inside information as to the Turkish Army. Accordingly Hamza adjusted his plans.

It had been a cloudy autumn evening, but at midnight the sky began to clear, with a bright moon and twinkling stars. They remained hidden in the wood, anxious about tomorrow.

Shabab was telling Hamza about a dream. 'I was somewhere – a riverbank – I was trying to get undressed, to jump in. Suddenly my lover came towards me. I grabbed my clothes. I tried to hide behind a rock. She kept on coming. I panicked. She saw me, and started laughing. Then, her tone suddenly serious, she told me to be careful, to look after myself. She wanted me back in one piece. My horse woke me neighing, and I was angry.'

They laughed, but now it was time to gird up for battle.

A refreshing breeze blew up when they started for enemy lines. They were divided into five groups, with each group assigned a leader. They began their assault at five a.m., with the enemy asleep. Drums, shouting and song, a strategy for panic and confusion, announced the attack. There was no let-up, when even those who attempted to escape were chased down and killed, all to the ringing out of the following battle song.

129

Brother, hit them, brother beat them,
Don't let them run,
You are cavaliers of Khanu's Dum Dum.
Don't let them run.
With God's help take your revenge.
They are cowards, looters of our homeland,
It is a high time we took our revenge.

They put a group of fighters in ambush over enemy retreat, and were incensed when a few stray Turks attempted to take women captives with them. They were caught. The women were saved. The men were summarily executed.

Seventeen Turks were killed, and twenty-two injured. Three Kurds died, and five were injured. Weapons, horses and the baggage from their trains were taken.

Back home, Dilbar was sick with worry, as there was no news from Shabab. She went to an old woman, a palm reader, to find out what had happened to him. The tiny shrivelled old crone took her hands in her own. 'Oh my dear, someone is trying to steal his heart,' she said.

That was not what Dilbar wanted to hear. She asked if he'd been killed or injured. 'Is he all right? Is he going to come back?'

The old woman stroked her hands gently. 'He is safe, but very far away. He is returning soon, in a week, ten days.'

Dilbar was relieved to hear that, and gave the old woman some silver coins.

On the day after the battle, the tribe and religious leaders gathered before Mir Sadiq's divan, in recognition of Hamza Chawesh. The people of Shamdinan were out early to see him, wanting to thank him and his men before their return to Dum Dum Castle. Mir Sadiq stood on a bench in the midst of the crowd, as if to make a speech, and turned to Hamza and his men.

'Our brothers, heroes of the castle, you have shown us your support. The occasion is unforgettable. You have saved us from Turkish aggression, and shown us a path to national unity. We are ready to repay you in whatever way we can.

God's peace be with you. My sincere compliments to our leader Khanu. God protect you all.' As a gift, he offered Hamza a sword in a golden sheath.

Hamza replied. 'Brothers and compatriots, it is our duty to defend our homeland. I am very happy and thankful to God that we have given you our support, and with minimum casualties The tribe of Dum Dum Castle is always ready for the front line. We shall not stand by and watch our enemies overrun our people. The failure of any of us is the failure of us all. We go back with pride, and take the news of our success to our leader. God protect you all. God's peace and grace be upon you.'

His warriors raised hands in salute, and as they were leaving the village an old woman came towards them. 'My dear, please, please tell me which one is Khanu Lap Zereen. I want to kiss him. I want to hug him. I have lost my son, but I sacrifice him and my soul to our great leader Khanu.'

One of the guards came forward. 'Sorry, so sorry. None of us is Khanu. He isn't with us.'

'God protect him. This is his army, and these are

the men who have saved us from the Turks.' The woman held up her hands and prayed to God for Khanu and his men.

Mir Sadiq had Hamza and his men escorted on the first leg of the journey back to the castle. The trip took them a week, but on the way they were treated by the villagers they met as liberating heroes, and were showered with gifts and other largesse. News of their success had spread, though many would often pause for the few young men they had lost.

It was in the era of Sultan Ahmet I, 1603–17 CE, when the Ottoman Empire faced both internal and external conflict. There was the Habsburg revolt in northern Hungary and Austria, a challenge to the sultan's authority. There was the Celali movement in Anatolia. Therefore, following defeat in Kurdistan, an immediate reprisal was not expected. The long wars in the Caucasus and northern Hungary were a drain on Ottoman resources.

The Celali movement came about because of mounting economic and social difficulties over the previous half century. The empire had spread from the Caucasus to Austria, and that had given rise to an extensive border that had to be controlled, often with great difficulty. One other significant problem was the rivalries between army leaders, with cavalry consisting of Turkmen, mostly from Anatolia, and the powerful Janissaries. The defeat of the Ottoman army near Lake Urmiya, on 5th September 1605, by Shah Abbas's army, and the revolt of a strong Kurdish clan of Canubulat in northern Syria, and the defection of several Kurdish and Turkmen leaders to the Iranian side, all conspired to weaken the Ottoman position. [See *History of the Ottoman Empire and Modern Turkey, the Rise and Decline of the Ottoman Empire 1280–1808*, by Stanford J Shaw, Cambridge University Press, pp182–9.]

As soon as they reached the castle, Shabab asked his sister Nanie to arrange a meeting with Dilbar as soon as possible. Dilbar wasn't at home, though her mother was. She suspected something. 'What's the matter? You come so early in the morning.'

Nanie wouldn't tell her the truth, saying, 'I have come to look at the new beads she has bought.' Then she changed the subject. 'Aunty, when did you get these beautiful carpets?'

'Last year, if I rightly remember, when merchants visiting Musa came here bearing gifts.'

Nanie stayed a little longer, in the hope that Dilbar would soon return. She didn't. Disappointed, she left. On her way home, she met her. 'My dear Dilbar, I was at your house. I have been waiting for you. Where have you been?'

'At my grandma's. She has been ill.'

'What is wrong?'

'I don't know. She says she has a chest pain. It might be her heart. Hakim (the local doctor) recommended honey, its wax mixed with olive oil. That is the only treatment available, and she can't eat fatty food.' Dilbar looked concerned.

'Why don't you take her to Sheikh Qasim? No one can treat anyone like him. Last year my brother fell ill, my father took him there, and he was cured. We paid a small piece of gold and sacrificed a sheep.

'My granny doesn't strongly believe in that. She says it's like witchcraft. Everything is up to God. No

135

one can oppose God's will.'

'Dilbar, I just came to tell you my brother is back. He wants to see you.'

Dilbar blushed and smiled, and even took a small mirror from inside her waistcoat to check her face. 'Tell him to go where I met him last time. I will be there tomorrow afternoon.'

'I don't think he can wait until tomorrow. He needs to see you today.'

'Then I will meet him after I've seen my uncle this evening. I'll be late, I'm afraid. I want to avoid being seen.'

After evening prayer, Shabab went to the designated place, but Dilbar wasn't there. She appeared only later, from the darkness of an alley. He rushed towards her, knowing this was not a proper place to do so. People were busy with their evening prayers.

He forgot his caution and opened his arms to her. They embraced, as if separation had been for years. Dilbar pushed him away, worried that someone might have seen them. 'There will be gossip all over

136

the castle. We'll never live down the shame. God knows what people will think.'

They decided to meet tomorrow, outside in the valley, where the merchants left their mules and horses, a pasture rich with oaks, acacias and mulberry trees, and alive to the sound of birds and the fluttering of butterflies.

Dilbar brought cheese, butter, honey and fresh bread, but they had no appetite. All they wished to do was lie with each other on the leafy turf, away from the castle's gaze. They stopped their talk. Their lips touched. She felt her heart quicken. He groaned with arousal, and their kisses grew more passionate. His heart pounded, and with strong insistent arms he drew her closer. Afterwards they slept. When he opened his eyes her beautiful face was fixated on his.

'It is so nice to be with you.'

'Yes. I was worried it would never be.'

Dilbar's sadness grew with each passing season. Each time he returned to her, it seemed only the prelude of departure, for there was always another war.

Shabab slept again. Dilbar looked around and caught a glimpse of two long snakes, entwined in each other, as if lovers. The scene so fascinated her, she was tempted to wake him, but didn't want to disturb him. But suddenly he opened his eyes. She kissed him on the forehead and showed him the snakes. He almost jumped to his feet, fearing they were poisonous, but Dilbar pushed his shoulder gently down, and did not to let him move.

He gently put his arm round her waist, and they kept watch until the snakes slithered into a thicket. Dilbar turned to him. 'When can we be free like them? Run around and go where we want? Just the two of us.'

'I thought we'd decided on next year,' Shabab said.

'Next year? I thought we said autumn,' Dilbar retorted.

'I can't marry before my sister,' Shabab reminded her.

'Then we will have to wait another year,' Dilbar replied, with a deep sigh of disappointment.

'We can run away together to my uncles. They won't let us down!'

'No, we can't do that. Our families get on well. We can't ruin that. Even with Khursheed's endless proposals, my father sticks to the line that you and I are made for each other.' She paused to tie a ring of tiny flowers in her hair, but bit her lip and shook her head. 'Do you really think we *are* for each other?'

Shabab looked at her awkwardly. 'Why ever not? Who can stop us?' He sounded so certain.

Dilbar loved to hear him say that and kissed him on the lips. 'You know, I'm just worried. So many wars. The Persians, the Turks – they never leave us alone. I'm so frightened.'

He held her hands. 'That is life, I'm afraid. War is a fact, and we have to stand up for ourselves.'

For Dilbar it was so sad, and the words echoed in her mind that life was just a war.

They walked off hand in hand, and in silence. It was getting late, and they had to go their separate ways. They departed after a few more kisses, and on to their respective homes.

139

Chapter Eight

By mid-autumn, the shepherds and farmers were coming down from the mountains, bringing with them their fodder and hay, their flocks and cattle, while others already in the villages were busy building new sheds, stores and houses, or with making general repairs.

Women contributed their share, retouching their interior house walls with a white soil mixture. They stocked up with sacks of charcoal and piles of wood for winter fuel, and with dried cattle dung, used as a fuel for cooking, with enough saved to burn on summer evenings as a repellent against insects, fleas and mosquitoes.

Since Khanu now had good control of the area, there were hardly any tribal conflicts over land trespass or property disputes. He would punish anyone who dared to undermine others' rights or infringe others' property or cause a nuisance of any kind.

Punishment was a heavy fine, with dismissal of any culprit found guilty of mistreating his neighbours or countrymen, and that meant banishment.

The villagers annually paid Khanu in money, gold or a percentage of their produce, as a tax for the castle's war expenses. People paid according to wealth or income. That apart, many would offer presents during religious and national festivities, to show their appreciation of Khanu's rule and leadership.

After Hamza's return, there were new military training sessions for the young. Hamza toured the villages, to persuade young men to join his training sessions, be that in the castle or in situ. Turkish prisoners who had been Kurds in the Ottoman Army were brought back as survivors of the Shamdinan battle and used in these training sessions.

After Shamdinan, there was a rumour that the Ottoman sultan and the Safavid king were to forge a pact for the division of Kurdistan between them, and would launch a campaign against Dum Dum Castle, so stung were they by the refusal of the Kurdish tribes to pay taxes and provide army recruits.

Shah Abbas ordered one of his ministers to take responsibility for forces sent to the castle. Kuli Khan was assigned to lead the new campaign, which was to start as soon as 2,000 warriors were ready and prepared. It took them two weeks of marching to get there, announcing themselves to the Kurdish villagers by their Persian cone-shaped hats and battle gear. They thought nothing of killing anyone who put up any resistance.

The villagers had no idea what was going on. A middle-aged well-built man with a light-brown beard sat astride a horse fronting twelve guards, four to the right, four to the left, and four to his rear. They slowed as the villagers gathered. They did not appear threatening – yet. Perhaps they knew where to meet the Kurds. When they came across a herd of sheep, an army captain ordered his men to seize it. A naïve young shepherd tried to resist, and when he went to complain was arrested. Orders from Kuli Khan were to collect all livestock along the way, with permission to kill anyone who stood up to them. Yet the villagers wouldn't give away their livestock easily. They would either retreat to higher ground or fight to the death, more often fleeing before the Persians' arrival.

The tribes were about to send for assistance, as they didn't know about the castle cavaliers a few miles away. Life was calm in the castle, with news of the Persian Army's advance well understood. There were extra defensive exercises well underway, led by the old fighter Zorab, who was a shrewd strategist with plenty of experience of fighting Persians. Khanu was always in touch with the situation.

These days, Khanu observed these training sessions more often, and was content with the way they were going. However, he wasn't sleeping well, as he worried about this new attack. When he did sleep, it was fitfully, till after seven each morning, when the sun was high. He missed morning prayer, while his wife had already been up for hours. One day two men were waiting for him at the divan. When his wife told him this he knew that the Persian Army had arrived.

143

'You should have woken me,' he said.

'You were dead to the world.'

He got ready and met his visitors.

'Al-salmun alaikum, God's peace on you.'

'Wa alikumasalam wa rahmatullahi wa barakatu, God's peace, mercy and grace on you, sir,' the two cavaliers replied. 'We have news that most of the Persians are cavaliers, sir. Our villagers have seen them. There were minor clashes. They were so many they sacked and plundered on the way.'

Khanu discussed options with his men, and they agreed to allow their aggressors into the mountains, where combat was easier, and there were plenty of opportunities for ambush, with trees, bushes, gorges, rocks. The villagers' natural propensity to withdraw to higher ground only lured the Persian Army where Khanu wanted them, with traps waiting.

He sent men to reconnoitre. Latest news was that the villagers were seeking shelter in the caves, while the scale of the Persian Army was barely known. They estimated about 2,000.

By now the castle fighters were ready. The divan

was not as crowded as usual, as many had retired for early-morning departure for the battlefield. Khanu was alone with one of his guests, Asoi Lakan, one of his best friends, and a man always willing to provide young recruits. He was the next strongest man in the area, looked up to and respected by all the tribes.

They didn't sleep until the small hours, spending their time planning the battle. They went out for a walk in the moonlight, under a twinkling of stars, when neighing and the tramp of horses' hooves suddenly shattered the peace. Their forces were gathering in the main square.

As dawn broke, people came out onto their roofs or stood before their houses, to wave off and weep for the brave young men. May God protect them. Under Khanu's leadership, 500 departed the castle, as meanwhile those villagers up in the mountain passes rained piles of rocks onto the Persian Army.

As Khanu's men neared the conflict, they divided into groups, an attack planned from both sides, left and right. Some were to withdraw tactically during the battle, to lure the Persians into traps, to cut them off from the main body of their army, and as isolated groups make them easier to finish off.

Khanu's division was to attack from the right, and Asoi Lakan's from the left, each with a group of 150. The rest were to wait behind with Hamza. Suddenly beating drums echoed in the valleys, as in the mythical story of the twelve cavaliers of Marivan.

The Persians were taken by surprise, some falling prey to the ambush as planned. Those lured into the chase were charged from behind, with many killed. Horses and weapons were seized. By the time news of the attack reached Kuli Khan, the Persian fighters were running scared, and withdrew. Khanu's oncoming fighters were joined by hundreds of Kurdish villagers, who together launched further attack. That caused panic among the Persians, who left their horses behind, as well as their weapons, rations and looted livestock. The corpse of a Persian commander was abandoned.

The main battle lasted for four days. The defeated army, demoralised, scattered in all directions, with villagers chasing after them. The Kurds lost twenty-six men, with twenty-five injured, from mainly those villagers who'd held up the Persians right at the beginning. Persian losses were high. They hadn't expected such ferocious reprisal at the hands of the Kurds.

The Persian King remained hopeful, but it was late autumn and cold weather was setting in. Attacks had decreased or stopped altogether, with snowfall hampering progress. A letter from the front stated, 'I doubt we are able to finish them soon. It has already been a few months. They never give us respite, and fight a guerrilla war. The rugged mountains and thick woodlands aid their resistance. It is scarcely conceivable we'll carry on through the winter.'

The king responded angrily. 'Hand me that letter!' he demanded. When someone did, he tore it to pieces, and asked for Saifullah Khan to be brought to him, who felt certain he'd be incarcerated, which was better than a return to battle. And indeed he was imprisoned for his incompetence.

Sardar Khan, one of the king's veterans, stood with his arms folded, listening. He was the king's

147

last choice, successful on many occasions, powerfully built, and having no remorse for the cruelty he'd enacted in the past. There was no doubting his loyalty to the king.

'Sardar, I'm sending you to take control. You have to do it your own way, whatever the cost. I want you to turn the castle upside down. Get Khanu alive and bring him here! Here before me! Is that clear! You have done it before! I know you can do it again!'

Sardar Khan bowed and withdrew three steps.

Back at Dum Dum Castle, life was beginning to get back to normality, its people returning to work. In Addi's house girls had gathered in groups to shear the sheep. The wool was washed in the river and dried in the open air, and later spun into threads for skilled workers to stitch into rugs, carpets, socks, hats, bedcovers and clothing material. Similarly trunks and ropes were made from goat hair.

Where the girls worked, the landlord provided food – nuts, sweets and dried fruit. The girls chatted all day long and joked, as there was plenty of gossip to pass the time. Playfully, they teased each other.

In Asfahan, Sardar Khan started to prepare an army in support of those already on the battlefield. His aim was for an army of 5,000 infantry and horsemen, all requiring rations. The procession towards Dum Dum Castle would take a few weeks, with many stops along the way. When he'd got his men there, he moved them into position.

Khanu wondered what was going on. One evening, when out with Jozow, he expressed his concern. 'The war has slowed. There's something in the air. We have to remain alert. I half expect a surprise attack.'

'Yes, I feel too there is something going on. We will soon see. I have warned everyone to be on the lookout.'

They were gazing out from the castle's eastern tower.

Back in Esfahan the king finalised urgent plans to speed up the pace of war and to destroy the castle. He intended to do so before the coming winter, but winter was making it almost impossible. Latest news was delivered by one of the king's men, in the form of another letter. It was handed to the king. The king asked one of his ministers to read it out. It said: 'God will protect our great king. I do not want to hide the reality of the situation in Kurdistan. Khanu's warriors are exterminating our men. The Kurds are popping up from everywhere, with guerrilla attacks on our fighters. The winter has set in. It makes the situation more difficult. So many of our men may freeze to death. We may have to postpone the campaign. Spring or summer would be better.'

Everyone went quiet. The king meditated briefly. 'Perhaps we have to wait. We need to address the situation properly. That man has built a formidable force. However, we must not rest until we have destroyed his castle and slaughtered his clan!'

The battlefield was quiet, apart from a few skirmishes now and then. Zorow, as one of the castle's group leaders, waved the others forward, mounted his white horse and led them over the crest. As they reached the valley floor the heat began to rise. The horses plodded on, heads down, their

150

hooves raising small plumes of dust, sweat streaking their flanks. The valley was dry and warm, or felt warm with its drying vegetation, a contrast to the cold weather the Persian Army was exposed to.

The going was slow, the afternoon wore on, and Shabab called out. Zorow looked back to see the injured Mardan had fallen off his horse. He was calling for the rest to stop and wait. Zorow swung his horse and rode to where the wounded man was struggling to rise. He dismounted and walked over to him, taking hold of his arm and hauling him to his feet. Mardan's eyes were glazed, his face ashen. Suddenly he doubled over, fell to his knees, and vomited.

Zorow stepped away from him, then looked around at the small group. The horses had little more in them, and the men were exhausted. 'How far to the pass now?' he asked Shabab.

'In the state we are in? Not before nightfall, I'd say.' The young man shrugged his shoulders.

To the right was a thick stand of mulberry trees. 'Ride in and see if you can find water. If we don't reach the pass in time, I know what might happen,' snapped Zorow!

Shabab rode off. Zorow helped Mardan to his feet and lifted him onto his horse. 'Don't fall off again, do you hear me!' Zorow said.

'I hear you,' mumbled Mardan.

'Let's get to the trees, it's cooler there,' Zorow shouted to his men.

Shabab found a hidden glade and led the group to it. There were boulders of white marble, and flowering bushes sprouting between the stones, their crimson blooms trailing down into a rock tank filled with cool water. The tank was fed by a stream cascading down over the boulders in a succession of tiny waterfalls. There was a good grass patch, and the glade was of such beauty that Zorow could almost believe that nymphs and dryads were hidden nearby.

The long cut to Mardan's skull had been patched, but the flesh was swollen and discoloured. Head wounds were always problematic. Zorow had once seen someone hit on the head but survive. Someone else had died with only the merest punch. Leaving Mardan to rest, the others attended their horses, using dried grass to wipe the sweat from their bodies, or leading them to the pool to let them drink.

As the men settled down in the shade, the horses feasted on the lush grass nearby. The men stripped of their armour and some jumped into the pool. The water was exquisite. One, on getting out, went so far as to say, 'A clear head and so much better. I had such a headache, as if a calf was trapped inside me, trying to kick its way out.'

'We only think of the dead when we're back home safe.'

Another fighter retorted: 'At last I will have peaceful sleep. I can't remember when I last did.'

Zorow lay down and tried to make himself comfortable. 'No worry. After I have slept, let the enemy come. I know I can kill that many you'll all lose count. But only after sleep.' He stretched out on the grass and closed his eyes.

It was dark when he woke. He looked around and saw the others fast asleep, apart from Shabab, who was in the pool, and Pestow sitting on a boulder, watching. He glanced at Mardan, the injured man. Bright stars were shining in the night sky. Mardan was on his back, apparently staring up.

'How's your head?' Zorow asked.

There was no response. Leaning over, he saw his eyes were closed, so got to his feet. He went to relieve Jozow on watch.

Hamza woke up, rubbed his eyes, his head pounding, his vision blurred. He tried to get up, and felt pain in his arms. His sword was smeared with blood. He examined his arms, and the injury didn't look serious, but why was it so painful? He dragged himself back to the boulder and sat upright against it.

He remembered the sword hammering against his helm. Five attacks they'd survived: in the first, the enemy couldn't get close enough, driven back by the volleys aimed at them. Then they regrouped with shields at their front, and advanced, still with arrows thudding into their arms, necks and legs. Zorow led a charge penetrating through their front line, and they fell back. The third attack had come sooner than expected and with more ferocity.

The day after the battle. The afternoon sun was strong, but a cool wind was blowing through the mountains as they rode on. The land was broad and open, rising and falling through gentle, wooded hills and gullies. High above Zorow saw a flight of ducks heading southwest towards a lake. He had always liked duck, especially grilled, and with herbs, and his stomach rumbled. 'It was just a dream.'

The castle recruits couldn't carry on fighting for much longer, with many wounded and killed. In the fourth assault the strategy changed, with enemy archers creeping forward, shooting up between the rocks and boulders. The Dum Dum warriors managed to pin them down.

In the fifth assault riders were lightly armed, and running out of ammunition trying to push uphill. They were driven back onto their own infantry, with many suffering broken bones as their horses kicked through their helms and breastplates.

At first they started their attack with confidence, but later, with many driven back, there were hardly

155

enough left to hold the narrow pass. Zorow looked up. There were a hundred horsemen who would like him to join them, but he was so tired he could hardly move, and was losing what little strength was left.

The clouds above the mountains were streaked with rusty orange from the dying sun. He was now lying on his back, staring at the sky, as a flock of birds passed by. At that moment he was jealous, wishing he too could fly high above the world and leave his worries behind.

He felt a pinprick in his chest. He touched it. His breastplate was broken, and blood was seeping out. At first he couldn't remember the incident, but gradually relived the stamping horse and the lance that struck him and knocked him back. Then there was not much fighting left – a few skirmishes here and there.

Chapter Nine

One morning, surrounded by his ministers, the king suddenly shouted: 'Bring me Hussein Khan.'

156

Hussein Khan was his father-in-law, whom he didn't like at all. He thought this might be the right time to get rid of him, though he wouldn't give his wife intimation of that.

Hussein Khan, on hearing he was summoned, couldn't help but worry. 'I hope it's nothing ominous.' But, curious, he responded immediately, and was soon at the palace kneeling before his king. The king's mood was to no one's surprise.

'Do you know why I asked you to come here?'

'No, Your Majesty, I am at your service, body and soul. Merciful God protect Your Majesty.'

'Have you heard what has been happening to our army in Kurdistan?'

'Yes, yes, certainly, Your Majesty, it is the most unfortunate news. But under Your Majesty's leadership we will soon overcome and defeat our enemy.' Hussein Khan was already offering his service. He had no other choice.

'Our army's defeat does nothing less than boost Khanu's confidence, and give him further credibility with the Kurds. We will wait until the winter is over, then launch a stronger attack and destroy the castle.'

'Certainly – Your Majesty's order will be implemented thoroughly. We will finish them off. Success is certain only under your command, with God's blessing and assistance.'

'Kulikhan was right, we should have waited till spring, when the roads are clear and the weather is warmer. It's your turn now. Let me see how soon you finish the job.'

'Yes, Your Highness, with God's help we will destroy them.' Hussein Khan was emphatic in his readiness to lead the attack.

Hussein Khan left the King and went to see his daughter, the king's wife.

'Are you all right, my dear father? God protect you, something must have happened.'

'Yes, yes, my dear. I'm fine. Nothing is the matter. I'm a bit unwell.'

His daughter suspected he'd been to see the king. 'You have met with Shah?' Her look was penetrating, as she awaited his reply.

'What can I hide from you, my dear? He just

ordered me to lead the army to Kurdistan, to Dum Dum Castle, to fight the Kurds. Kulikhan's army has been shot to pieces, and *he* was killed.'

No, father, he can't do that, he can't send you. I won't let him do it.'

Hussein Khan knew she couldn't stop him, and anyway he didn't want her involvement.

'There's nothing you can do, my dear. I don't want you to talk to him about it. I have to do what I'm told. If I am seen to plead with the king through you, I'll be branded a coward.'

'No, I insist. He can't send you. There are so many he *can* send. His aim is quite obvious – to get rid of you.' She wept on his shoulder.

Her father tried to disengage himself, and at last pushed her away. 'Listen, my dear, listen! It is not the end of the world. I have been in so many wars before, and with God's mercy I will survive this one. Don't worry. I will be all right.'

'I may never see you again.'

'Don't you dare mention the subject to him. He will have me killed. You know how he hates me. I don't want to cause problems, so don't interfere.'

'But he could so easily send someone else. There are plenty of eager youngsters.'

'Don't worry, I will be fine.'

The lower mountain reaches were blanketed with woodlands and orchards, with the latter owned by the villagers, and well looked after. The hilly slopes had been excavated, and buttressed with rocks to prevent rainwater washing away the soil. These steep, bench-like walls were supported by plantings to bind the soil.

In winter, when the wool work was underway, Shabab's family was one of those often in need of assistance. The whole community worked together, with Dilbar one of the girls always ready to help. Shabab always looked forward to it, wanting to see her. He asked his sister, 'Didn't you say Dilbar was coming?'

She looked at him and smiled. 'Later in the evening, brother. Don't worry, she will come – with all the girls.'

Evening arrived, and he couldn't hide his anxiety.

'Nanie, how come they are so late?'

'The first evening's like that. They come to be shown what to do. On the following days they will come earlier.'

At last they came in twos and threes, with Dilbar the last to arrive. Shabab got up as soon as he saw her.

The girls glanced at each other with a smile and a wink. Dilbar knew what they meant. One of the girls raised her voice: 'He is not bold enough. Other young men are not like him. They prepare nuts and sweets for their girls.' The others teased as well.

Shabab, embarrassed, didn't say anything. He went to the Jewish kiosk and bought sultanas, nuts and grilled chickpeas, and gave them to his sister for the girls.

'You have been quite unfair to my brother. Look what he has brought for you,' Nanie said.

The young girls giggled, teased and shouted when Nanie's mother came.

'Salaam, my dears. Thank you for your assistance. Tonight we will clean the wool. Then we pick out the straws. Then comes the spinning. But please do work at your leisure. Thank you again for coming.'

After three days working on the wool, and on the final day, it was customary to hold festivities: dancing, singing, games, with the landlord cooking for them. There was music, the drum and Zorna's flute, and Muraz the castle singer. The girls loved his presence. Whenever he played the Nerjis flower tune, two girls and two boys accompanied.

'The Nerjis flower, the flower of love,
Your smell, your sparkling dew, your beauty is for us,
From early spring until summer comes.
On the plains, in the mountains, under a golden sun,
By rivers and streams,
In the vast plain's wealth, lush in its green.'

He repeated the tune several times, then started to sing again.

Kurdistan, Kurdistan, full of mountains,
Kurdistan, Kurdistan, full of valleys and plains.
Kurdistan, Kurdistan, you change your dress
With every season filled with happiness.
So full of life, and pied in beauty,
As we see in the smiles of every girl and boy.
Kurdistan, Kurdistan, we all dearly love
You, so beautiful heaven knows above.
May the mighty God damn the Turkish Ottoman,
And all the Persian kingdoms.

Neighbours, families and friends were all there to
enjoy the party. Dancing varied from place to place
in Kurdistan, but in most cases participants formed a
line and held hands at hips, and as one swayed
backwards, forwards, sideways, with others joining
in or dropping out as fancy took them. Other
attractions were music, poetry and storytelling,
mostly in celebration of the beauty of Kurdish
women or the redoubtable deeds of Kurdish heroes,
ancient or modern. [See *Family of Man Magazine*,
vol 5, part 1, pp1694–97.]

163

It went on until late in the night, the revellers blissfully unaware of a large Persian army fighting its way towards the castle. At Khanu's divan, the mood was totally different. There latest news was that a fresh Iranian attack was imminent, whose object was to destroy the castle and subjugate its people.

Khanu knew that facing this new threat wouldn't be easy. He had no backing from anywhere, apart from his own tribe and villagers. The battle would be decisive – they'd survive, or they wouldn't. He had no thought of surrendering to the Persians. His first step was to prepare 400 scouts-cum-combatants to monitor the movement of the advancing army at close range, and send back intelligence. On his side, Hussein Khan was preparing his new division.

The army, on moving out, was so large it took a whole day to leave Asfahan. It was mid-spring, with the mountains still subject to snow. The Safavid Army, huge and well equipped, was also on its way. Hussein Khan planned an unexpected attack, but had to revise that tactic when he didn't take into account the villagers' loyalty to Khanu. There was also the unpredictability of the weather and the rugged mountains. It was, too, the case that Dum Dum Castle was so well fortified it was likely to withstand a siege for a very long time.

'Unless we can find a way to open the gates.'

Hussein Khan had often used traitors to gain information, but the problem here was how to find one.

Perhaps after all they would lay siege and starve Khanu's people into surrender. But, the weather was getting worse, with continuous rain followed by a snowstorm. They came into mountains where in many places there was only a narrow path. It was easy to lose one's footing.

A few subordinates started to question the route plan. Hussein Khan fretted too, and began to doubt his Kurdish guide. He gave orders for the man to be brought before him.

'You may guess why I asked for you. It is impossible to pass through the mountains. What have you to say?'

'I am a faithful servant of the empire. Everyone has trust in me. I couldn't let anyone down, especially the emperor. No one can do anything about the weather. I know this country like the palm of my hand. We need patience. We cannot proceed in bad weather.'

As Hussein Khan was not yet reassured, he didn't give the order to stop. Then came news of losses, of men, horses and mules on one of the mountain passes. That was another dent in the guide's credibility.

'I thought I could trust you. Your service to the empire is long.'

'I have betrayed no one. I am loyal to the empire.'

'You have deceived me. What can you say? We have lost men, and are likely to lose more.'

'I have been in His Majesty's service for much of my life. I have never done wrong. Now you accuse me of treason.'

'You lie to me! You have put us in a trap. Traitor! Out of my sight!'

Guards closed in, and the guide had no alternative

but to draw his sword. He fought bravely and skilfully, disarming one of them, whereupon he tried to escape. He slipped and fell as others set about him and managed to pin him down. Immediately six or seven swords were pointed at his heart, head and stomach.

Hussein Khan gave the command: 'Finish him off!'

He was rained with sword strokes, and his head was cut off. Hussein Khan's next order was to withdraw the regiment and get out of here. The result of that was a clash with the fighting forces sent from the castle, who'd been watching their every move. They beat them into retreat.

News of it reached the king, who ordered Hussein Khan's return to Asfahan. Again he was required to bow and kneel before his king, whose mood was stern.

'Well now. An explanation, I think....'

'God protect Your Majesty. Everything went well, until we reached the foot of the mountains. There was a heavy snowfall. When we tried to take a short

167

cut, to surprise the castle with a sudden attack, we found we were stuck. There was no way through.'

'What about your guide?'

'He was a traitor, God forbid. He laid the trap that led us into the high mountains, with no way out.'

'No, that can't be true. He was faithful to me. He fought for us in many wars.'

'God protect Your Majesty. He made no attempt to get us out. The situation was critical.'

'Bring me the guide.'

All he got was the head. He gave orders not to let his family know what had happened, and from now on his only preoccupation was to overrun the castle. There was a new plan for an attack in the following spring.

Chapter Ten

Shah Abbas gave consent for all necessary measures for a final assault on the castle. Weapons, including cannons, had been brought by Europeans, who were training his men. He moved to regain lost territories, first smashing the Uzbeks and capturing Heart, Mesh and Merv in Transoxania (1588 CE) and, after negotiating with Spain and Portugal, recapturing Azerbaijan and Caucasus from the Ottomans (1603–04).

Ottoman efforts to resist Safavid invasion were undermined by lack of discipline and poor leadership. Shah Abbas's rout near Lake Urmiya (5th September 1605) left him in a good position to move deep into eastern Anatolia.

Khanu thought back over all the battles. The losses endured by his men were high. For the Persians, life was cheap, but not for him – his soldiers were his kinsmen. They were few, while the Persians had added ever more.

Khanu began to see the world in a different

169

perspective. He reflected on so many years of power, as if that power was approaching its end. His world was almost over.

He saw that the Kurds' lack of unity would lead them to a life of submission and subjugation. He knew that with all the Kurds behind him he would fight back fiercely, against both the Persian and the Ottoman Empire. But for now it looked at an end, like the lost brilliance of summer or a last crimson sunset.

His household was busy, as were all in the castle and villages. Saifadin, his elder son, stood by him, especially in these hard days, and with the approach of war. Khanu's lesson for him was one of tribal relations, leadership, how to keep the people together, unity, the importance of togetherness in face of the enemy. He put emphasis on patience. His son had been educated at Tabrez, where he learnt Arabic, Turkish and Persian. Khanu had committed him as a leader and sent him into battle, where he had gained valuable experience fighting alongside castle veterans.

The market was busy, with herds of cattle brought for sale. Khanu's surplus of livestock had been assigned to his sons, who would bargain for the best price, with a need to raise money for the war effort. Khanu himself had sent for his leaders, and the divan was crowded with guests. He addressed them.

'You may already know, my brothers, why I have sent for you. We all know that Shah Abbas's huge army will attack the castle. With God's help we'll repulse them.'

'We will, with the assistance of merciful God,' one of his guests put in.

'In the last two years, Shah (the king) has attacked us twice. This will be his third assault, with thousands more infantry and cavaliers.' There was a solemn air of silence as he paused. 'On the other side of the border the Turks attack us too, so now with them and the Persians we shall have to fight to the very last man. We prefer death to submission.'

News of the attack spread everywhere: to the

171

mosques, the market, the teashops and the fields. It was explained by Mullah Rasheed in Friday prayer, at the castle mosque, when he dealt with the Persian king's attempt to convert them to the Shiite sect. He encouraged his congregation to fight back. Anyone killed would be a martyr. The general view was that Shah Abbas wanted to expand his power to the Kurds, and in bringing them under his control exact taxes and recruit soldiers for his wars.

Khanu knew how much the last defeat of their army and the loss of their leader had angered the king, and that revenge would be bloody. He assigned a part of his preparation to Hamza, with divisions of cavaliers and infantry. More villagers volunteered for training, bringing rations, money, weapons, horses.

The town was turned into an army barracks, with hundreds of men requiring weapons, which ranged from bows and arrows, to spears, shields, swords, lances, chains. There was a group of women trained to provide rations, to prepare food, and to ensure water, and for medical treatment. They were accommodated in the castle, with some located in camps in the rearguard of the battlefield.

Khanu was pleased with what he saw, with hundreds of new recruits arriving all the time. At one of the weapon distribution points in the southwest, even untrained villagers came to receive arms.

'How long do we have to wait?' a middle-aged man shouted.

'Whose group are you? If you're not registered, we can't give you weapons.'

'What do you mean? When the enemy comes, they don't ask us whose group we are. They slaughter us. I don't belong to any group. I belong to the nation. Give us weapons.'

The supervisor explained the procedure. 'Listen, Haji, we have to be organised. Each of us is assigned to a different division. We can't just give away weapons to anyone. But you're right, the enemy does not differentiate between us. Understand, it is not a tribal conflict. It's a war, and we have to be organised. We cannot fight back without a proper system, without a plan, without leadership. God bless you, go and find your group and register for weapons. Come back and see me later.'

News reached the castle that the Persian Army was on the move again – an enormous force. Everyone gathered in the castle to finalise plans with the war committee. In the meantime Khanu sent Shabab with a group of men to establish the Persians' exact location, size, leadership etc.

He met with Dilbar before his departure. He didn't wait to ask his sister to call her, and went by himself to the house. She greeted him with a smile.

'I hope there's nothing wrong. You've come by yourself.' She had never seen him at her home on his own.

'It's nothing. I'm about to check on the advance of the Persian Army.'

'Oh my God, is it war again? Damn the king. They never leave us alone.'

'No, they don't.'

'Is it a big army, as they say?'

'That's what I have to find out.' He was trying to reassure her.

'I want to join the women's division, but my parents won't let me. It's crazy. We want to be trained, and join the men. What is our value after we lose our heroes?'

'We have already too many young men in the army. There is no need for you to get involved. The situation isn't that desperate.'

He made to go. Dilbar called him back. 'Shabab, wait a minute. I almost forgot to give you something.'

'I need nothing. I have got all I need.'

'Please, wait a minute. I have prepared a dua [a triangular piece of a material in a colourful wrapping, to stick under his arm for protection]. I paid the mullah to write it for you. Please keep it with you, it includes verses from the Koran. I hope God will protect you. I'll get it for you.' She hurried in quickly to get it, and didn't let him go until she'd pinned it under his arm. She put her hands round him and called his name: 'Shabab, Shabab, my God.' She was thinking about their future, which didn't now look promising. 'You have got a chain on you. It will strengthen your protection. I pray to God to protect you, Shabab. I'm very frightened. I don't know, this time is not like before. May God destroy those evil forces, the Persians and the Turks.'

'We will just have to face it. This has never been a peaceful world for us. We are defending our dignity. We are proud of our willingness to fight back. We are ready to die for our country.' As he whispered these words, Dilbar was on the verge of tears.

'Stop that! It is not the first time I'm going to war. I want you to be strong. If I see you again in this state, I won't call on you again.' He left without looking back. He was in the flush of youth, and never doubted himself.

Discussion in the divan lasted until almost midnight. There were suggestions, but no specific plan had been reached. Khanu had weighed it all up.

'We already know why Shah Abbas attacks us almost every year. He wants to collect taxes. He wants his army recruits. He wants us to change our religion to Shiism. It is all quite clear.'

'Yes, it is absolutely clear. We have attacked no one. We just want to live in peace, God protect you. We are all behind you,' an elderly man responded.

The next speaker was Hamza, the castle's distinguished commander. 'We understand Shah Abbas's true intention. This time it is a fight for survival. In all other attacks we have defeated him. In the last war we killed Kuli Khan, his army leader. This time he has put together the most capable men in his army. He intends to uproot us, slaughter our children, seize our homeland, loot our properties. What will be left to live for?' He looked for, and got, gestures of support. 'It is the same with both Ottoman and Persian armies. We have no alternative but to fight, and by any means not let them encroach on our land while we are here to defend it. We fight to the last man.'

The outcome was this. All decided to devote whatever was at their disposal to fight the coming war. Its preparation was already underway, but the purpose of the meeting had been to form an unbreakable solidarity under the leadership of Khanu. The main counsellors of war were: Hamza, Jozow, Saifadin, Askander, Asoi Lakan and Khanu.

The mood of the town had already changed from bustling good cheer to sombre introspection. Khanu sat astride his grey horse and inspected his troops. The chief mullah and the religious leader Sheikh Jalal were on their way to express support.

'Our leader, our great leader, we are all behind you body and soul. We plead with the mighty God to protect you from the enemy's evil intent.'

Khanu charged his horse towards them and looked straight at them. 'I will have more satisfaction in your words if you join us and give incentive to our warriors,' he said, raising his voice to make himself heard.

'I swear to God, we will join you, we will. Our

survival is bound to your success. Who would turn away from sacred duty? Our life is never more precious than yours, our great emir!'

The warriors started to depart. At the front was Khanu, emblazoned with yellow flags. The old veteran Askander was just behind him, then came the spears division, and after that bows and arrows and swords.

The army comprised age groups fourteen to sixty-five, mixed, youth with experience. The procession lasted two hours, and four hours later they were well away from the castle. Khanu gave instruction to stop and take a rest, as the infantry divisions needed to catch up.

They pulled up near a spring, a normal resting place for the caravans of merchants, and a rich pasture for their horses. Khanu turned to Jozow.

'Look, the infantries are almost left behind. They can't get tired so soon. A tired army cannot fight. It will be defeated.'

While Khanu bathed in the spring, he saw some of his men on horseback, approaching in a cloud of dust. 'It must be Shabab. He flies like the wind on his horse.'

Shabab was drenched with sweat and climbed down quickly.

'We haven't come across the Persian Army yet, but news from the villagers suggests they are near,' he said.

'I did not send you to bring others' gossip,' Khanu admonished. 'I want you to go and see for yourself.'

Hamza added his opinion. 'Did I train you to work like this?'

'No sir, I'm sorry. I go back immediately.'

It took him a few hours to return to the checkpoint. He and his comrade Pestow, a big bulky man, stopped to rest. They drank from a stream. The day was calm, the breeze was light, small herds of sheep were clustered round the trees.

'Oh my God, look, Shabab, they are so many.' Pestow had climbed a hill and was looking down at the Persians.

§

Askander, the head of infantry, was the first to arrive

from the group of stragglers. Jozow turned to him. 'If you get tired so soon, how can we fight?' It was now obvious Askander was too old for this.

Khanu told his men to get him a horse, but at first he wouldn't accept it. 'I am not weaker than the rest of our men.'

Khanu insisted. 'You can't carry on like that for the next few months. You are not a young man anymore. Don't worry about the rest of them, they are all well trained.'

'Your words are final and indisputable, sir. God protect you.' He accepted the offer and was grateful to Khanu. When a horse was brought he tried to climb on, but it wouldn't stand still. Askander took a firm hold of the bridle and mounted, and once in the saddle waved his sword above his head, which made the young warriors laugh.

'He doesn't need training like you,' said Khanu. 'He is one of our most experienced warriors.'

The mood lightened, with Khanu even surprised at the little anxiety there was.

'Did the musicians come with us?' he asked.

181

'Yes, they are here,' Jozow replied. Some had brought flutes.

Khanu asked for Muraz and Moorid to play.

Dancers formed a line, and the warriors joined in, their swords held up vertically before their faces. The choir sang, 'Nabie, nabie, nabie to the enemy' (meaning no, no, no to the enemy).

Khanu joined the chant:

'Nabie, nabie, nabie to our enemies,
Nabie to the Persians.
We won't give in to Shah Abbas,
We will fight to the last man,
We will fight, we will fight as long as we can
For our leader. We won't give up, we won't give
in,
To the last man we will fight as long as we can,
To the last man.'

Khanu smiled defiantly, proud of his men. The whole thing lasted until their evening meal. Then they were back on the road again and on their way.

But it was nightfall, and they could hardly see before their feet, and everyone was quiet. There was only the sound of horses' hooves.

The following morning, Zorow and his men chanced on a group of Persians moving out into the open from below a cliff edge. There were over thirty of them, following a path. In the lead was a short slim man, in a cloak of faded brown. The slope was steep. Zorow gauged it was about 250 paces.

'You see that little group of boulders on the hillside? We'll hit them there when they reach the rocks. If they break and run, we'll give chase before we ride on. If not, they'll charge, and we'll hit them – hard. When you see my signal, follow me, and spread out.'

They crept into a better shooting position, while Zorow remained quite calm. Notching their arrows to their bows, they waited.

The thirty-odd Persians approached in due course. They were closely packed and were chatting to one another, obviously not expecting to be ambushed.

183

The castle warriors were outnumbered three to one, yet still expected the Persians to flee. The moment they came before them, Zorow stood up and fired an arrow at the leader. It missed, but hit the man behind him in the arm. Soon a volley of arrows struck more, and four Persians fell. The rest charged rather than fled, but Zorow's men were ready. He aimed another arrow. It punched through the skull of its target, and the man fell back, and rolled down the slope. The group kept to their cover behind the boulders, but the Persians were getting closer. More of them fell. Zorow dropped his bow and drew his sabre, and his dagger. Undeterred, the Persians continued to advance, and now it was face-to-face combat.

Zorow was leapt on, but ducked under the blows that followed, and plunged his sword into the man's chest, rounding off with a head butt. As the man fell back he tore his sword clear of his body. He lashed out at a second man, his sabre slicing through the flesh of his arm. Then came Pestow charging in, followed by Shabab, stabbing and slashing at a group

184

now surrounding Zorow. A blow struck his helm, spinning it clear. He swung round, half dazed, and launched himself at his attacker. The two collided and hit the ground. Zorow scrambled up then drove his sword into the man's skull. The blade stuck fast. Letting go of the hilt he spun around – just in time to parry a thrust from a spearman. He grabbed at the spear and dragged the man towards him, kicking his legs from under him. As the man fell Zorow thrust his dagger into his neck.

Another soon charged at him, sword raised, but Pestow pierced him with his sabre, and the man fell, blood spurting from his torso. Zorow acknowledged the debt, while Pestow returned a cheeky grin. When the Persian group leader was killed, and with many of his comrades dead or dying, the rest fled, abandoning their weapons. Zorow handed Shabab his helm, who was so dazed he hadn't seen it had fallen off. He looked around for his men. Pestow was sitting on a boulder with a cut to his head, and blood smearing his face. Shabab combed the battlefield,

185

examining the dead and wounded. Some of the Persians had fallen down the valley, but he didn't bother to check on them. Two of their own were dead, with five injured, but their leading soldiers were not seriously harmed. Zorow looked rather grimly at a man with his throat torn open, then stripped him of his armour. He walked round and counted enemy losses. Two had been carrying packs with supplies – bread, butter, cheese, purloined from the Kurdish villagers.

'Time to eat,' he said. He tore off chunks of bread and shared it round. Thereafter they took whatever else was useful left on the battlefield. Next they interrogated what wounded Persians hadn't got away – some slivers of information there.

The midday sun blazed in a clear sky, but a cool wind was blowing through the mountains. Shabab removed his helmet, allowing the breeze to cool his head.

'A nice day's work,' Zorow said.

§

It had been a few days since Shabab was sent on his mission. He came back with two prisoners, and was invited to break bread with Khanu. Hajow, a castle guard, was surprised to see him again.

'Marhaba Shabab, you are back so soon,' he said with a sarcastic smile.

'You should not pass judgement,' said Khan. 'Shabab and his men have overcome a group of Persians and taken two prisoners.'

'Then where are they?' Hajow asked.

'You will see soon enough,' answered Shabab.

Khanu and his son were impressed by his achievement, and presently the prisoners were brought before them. They were hungry, tired and subdued, and clearly the worse for recent interrogation, as their bruises and scars attested.

'It is not our custom to beat and harm our prisoners,' Khanu said. 'That's provided they make no attempt to escape.'

One of them was lanky and middle-aged, and the other young, shortish and with curly brown hair. At first they didn't want to answer questions, and had to

187

be threatened with torture. The younger man pleaded for his life, and soon gave in to the investigation.

'Our army is 30,000, led by Hussein Khan. Mission is a final onslaught on the castle. We have all kinds of weapons. Gunpowder, artillery. We have thousands of cavaliers. Our instructions are to kill anyone who stands in our path.'

§

With the castle warriors on the move again, there many more villagers trying to escape to higher ground, taking their livestock with them. When asked of the situation, an old man spoke.

'The Persians are at it again. We worry they will slaughter all of us.' He looked exhausted. They had left behind men and women older than himself, also the disabled and infirm. Crops had been left un-harvested.

Khanu's men marched forward into a bank of cloud building up on the horizon. It turned to thunder, and a storm with torrential rain, which when it stopped saw Shabab on his way again. The Persians were near, and could be seen from where

Khanu and his veterans had situated themselves in the mountains. The Persian force was enormous.

Khanu considered his strategy. Sotow looked worried. 'I am not exactly a novice,' he said, 'but I have never in all my days seen so large an army.'

'You worry now,' Assoi Lakan said sarcastically. 'We haven't even started!'

'No doubt,' Sotow replied. 'They're even massing on the other side of the hill.'

'That's a route we have to block,' Khanu added.

'I will go there,' Askander volunteered. Khanu glanced at him without a word.

It was agreed that the first attack would be three-pronged: from the right Assoi Lakan, from the left Hamza, from the middle Sotow. Askander was disappointed at not having a role, and was counselled by Khanu.

'Askander, I want you with me. I shall need a few hundred waiting at the ready. Swapping in and out will be our best chance. I see no other way of taking on so large an army. Our numbers don't even add up to a fifth of theirs.'

189

'It is not the number, it's the quality,' Askander replied.

'In this case, it's number *and* quality,' Khanu corrected, then addressed the entire assembly. 'We are now very close, so close they could attack us any time they wanted – if they knew we were here. We must withdraw our infantry – at the moment it's an easy target. That will also make space behind us, room for us to manoeuvre into. We cannot attack from any single front. We have to disperse and surprise them from different directions. We cannot face them head on. They are so many they will simply overwhelm us. It's a fight for survival, but we pray God's help. Merciful God protect you all.'

They decided to launch their attack early in morning, with the enemy still asleep, using the guerrilla tactics they had learned so well. Supply lines couldn't be depended on, so water would have to be carried. For now they must rest, with a guard posted. The situation was tense.

The conflict had its competing points of view. One interpretation was of an empire driven by pressure of population and the need to acquire new territory. On the other hand, the castle's warriors came with a strong impulse to defend what was theirs – their land, their families, their property. Not one of them had been called to arms by force. They had taken to war in a profound sense of their destiny. They could not think of defeat.

§

Khanu, flitting in and out of sleep, woke suddenly to find his son Saifadin nearby. He had seated himself near some rocks.

'You sleep ill, father.'

'It's a difficult day ahead. Who can I turn to for help?'

There were other Kurdish leaders, such as Tagur, Shikak and Shamdinan, whom he might have sounded out. He wondered now if it was a mistake not to have.

Just after midnight he gave the order for everyone

to be woken and prepared for battle. They rumbled into action with a hammering of horses' hooves and the beat of drums, attacking on all sides, with surprise their main weapon. Pestow leapt into the fray, knocking one soldier off his feet. An arrow lodged in the throat of another. There were sword thrusts, a shoulder charge, lots of hacking, slicing, and a river of blood.

Khanu watched from the hillside, pleased with progress so far. He noticed a large chain of Persians trying to encircle the Kurds, and instantly ordered a counter-attack, sending in his son to regroup the three divisions. He saw through a break in the trees the first rank of the enemy line. There were heavily armoured warriors, with shields. Another group on the left were kitted out with leather breastplates, and were equipped with spears and swords.

A battle cry went out from enemy ranks, and there was a charge towards the Kurdish line. Khanu got off his horse with his shield and sword at the ready, and immediately saw his men outnumbered – the ration

192

roughly ten to one. Hundreds raged across open ground, with blood-curdling battle cries. A volley of arrows ripped through them, but it didn't slow their advance.

Hundreds nudged their horses forward. Hamza ducked under a hanging branch, leading the way. The bright morning sun reflected off the armoured riders moving to the hillside. Pointing his spear, Asoi Lakan charged head-on with his group at full gallop. They were close enough to see the panic in their enemy's faces. They slammed into the horde of Persians. Zorow rammed his spear through the chest of one. As the man fell off his horse, he drew his sabre, slashing wildly. All was chaos. The air was filled with the screams of the wounded and dying. Hamza drove his gelding on, deeper into opposition ranks. An axe blade cleaved the gelding's neck and it fell.

The Persians seemed to be retreating. Khanu, Jozow and Saifadin took up their positions of ambush.

'This is the crucial moment,' Khanu said, and wished them success. One thousand of Saifadeen's men were assigned to climb trees on the withdrawal route, and began their attack as the Persians retreated, right into their ambush. Khanu watched as they were caught from both sides, and was especially impressed with Jozow and his son, fronting the column of attackers. Panic ensued, and a stampede, whereupon Zorow drove deeper into enemy ranks.

He was charged, but he jumped clear, launching himself at an axe man. There was no time to bring up his sword, so a head butt sufficed, and the Persian was sent staggering back. Then came another parry at him, as riders closed around him. He tried for a riderless horse, but it reared up and galloped away. Two Persians rushed at him. The first swung an axe, which he tried to block with his sabre.

The blade shattered. Zorow hurled the hilt at the second man, who ducked. The axe man raised his weapon again. Zorow charged at him, grabbing the shaft, and ramming his head into the warrior's face.

The warrior fell back, losing his grip on the axe. Zorow swept it up, and with a bellowing war cry leapt towards the second warrior. The man's nerve broke and he tried to run. Pestow suddenly appeared, plunging his lance into the warrior's back.

Zorow ran to a fallen rider. Dropping the axe, he took up the man's sabre and hurled himself back into the fray, hacking, slashing and stabbing. They enemy were hardy and tough, but they had little training. They fought as individuals, seeking space to swing their swords, or use their spears and axes. They found themselves crushed by a mass of highly organised battlefield vets.

Desperate to find room, they began to peel away, running for open ground. The castle warriors were waiting to cut them down. The horde began to scatter, its army sundering apart. Now the slaughter began.

Panic swept through the Persians, who began to flee. Horsemen rode after them, cutting and killing. Hamza saw horseless Zorow striding towards him, his helm and breastplate smeared with blood, his sword arm crimson from wrist to elbow.

'You hurt?'

'No.'

'Then help with the wounded.'

Zorow cleaned his sword and slid it back into its scabbard. He gazed around the battlefield. Victory was complete, but their losses were high. He worked alongside the stretcher-bearers until almost dusk. By that time he had carried at least a hundred corpses. The enemy's dead were nearly double that. Their armour and weapons were stripped, for redistribution among themselves.

Prisoners were rounded up and interrogated. Zorow watched, and though he could not hear he read what was said in their surly faces. Khanu did not accept torture as an instrument of war, if prisoners were willing to give information. Most men would tell you anything at the threat of castration, or the putting out of eyes, but there was no need for that.

Hamza had witnessed the way Zorow ripped through enemy lines, like an angry tiger, as he later described it. The fight had lasted almost a day, and Khanu knew they could not face a never-ending Persian army, even when falling like autumn leaves. They would still keep coming in the hundreds and thousands.

Pressure was building up on him and his warriors. He had no choice but to withdraw to higher ground, where they had laid more traps for the Persians. The Persians pursued them, and again opened themselves to guerrilla attack.

'I'm leaving these for you,' Khanu said to Hamza. To the Persians, the Kurds seemed to pop up everywhere.

At sunset news came of Pestow's death. He had been seen surrounded by Persians, fighting bravely to the last. He was later rescued, badly wounded in the stomach, but died on the way back to the castle. His and other corpses had been brought to Khanu's camp, wrapped in a blanket.

'We must all be ready for sacrifice, in defence of our country. Pestow's is one of the finest examples

197

of gallantry. God's prayers on his soul,' Khanu said. Prayers were read for the others too.

In light of this fierce resistance, the Persians brought in reinforcements by the thousands. Khanu ordered his army not to give chase, a wise tactic given the growing ferocity of the Persians, who razed every village they retreated through. Homesteaders were burnt alive in their houses, while civilians on the streets were cut to pieces. That made the Kurds even more defiant and angry.

News reached the king (Shah Abbas) that the war was far from over, with heavy losses moreover. He anticipated the destruction of Dum Dum Castle very soon. He ordered his commanders to send more troops from the Qizlbash area. The war dragged on for months. The rank and file of the Persian Army began to curse the terrain and the rugged mountains. But nobody could question the king's motive for war.

The king thought to trick Khanu. He sent one of his tribal leaders to negotiate a ceasefire with him, with the promise that he alone would be recognised as leader of all Kurds, and an amnesty. In exchange he was to swear his fealty to the Persian Empire.

Khanu refused. 'We are not the aggressors. We have not come to occupy his country. We have not come to slaughter his people.' Khanu's message to the king was clear and concise.

With that exchange of messages underway, the Persian Army planned another attack on the castle, this time from a different front. When Khanu learned of it, he sent Askander and his division, and reinforcements of 600 men. Shabab liaised between the different groupings. He was put in charge of the exchange of warriors, of conveying the injured to the castle, and of providing provisions to the front line. Early one morning, he detected movement in the valley, close to Askander's headquarters.

He told Askander what he had seen, and climbed down with a group of cavaliers. One of them shouted: 'Who are you, speak! Speak before you are killed!'

'We are sent by the king. We seek parley with Khanu.'

Askander made his men tie their arms, and had them taken away. When Khanu was informed of this, he summoned the intruders immediately.

'Where do you come from? Who sent you? What do you want?'

'Thanks be to God, sir, we have come to deliver a message from Shah Abbas. We are honoured to see you. Shah Abbas is sending you his words. He swears to mighty God that he will recognise you as leader of all the Kurds. He will cease hostility, as soon as you confirm your loyalty. He will send 2,000 pieces of gold.' The two men remained kneeling. 'Shah Abbas wants your answer, sir.'

'Go back to your king and tell him I'm a Kurdish Khan, not a Persian Khan. I don't want his gold. Tell him to stop slaughtering our people. It is our homeland and we will fight for it to the last. If he is serious, tell him to withdraw and we will talk.'

The war was into its fourth month when the messengers reached Asfahan. The king got up from his chamber and started to shout. 'How? How is it that mountainous Kurd does not listen? I swear, I will destroy his castle!' His voice was heard all over the palace.

He started on his ministers. 'Send more troops, more troops. His castle must be destroyed before the coming winter. Is that clear?' Everyone bowed.

He turned to Sardar Khan, one of his trusted army veterans. 'Sardar, I will send you to take control and lead the army. You must succeed, whatever the cost. Turn the castle upside down and bring Khanu before me. Bring him alive. I know you can do it.'

Sardar Khan stepped a few paces back, and bowed to his king.

As soon as Sardar Khan and his army reached the battle zone, he took over leadership, while Khanu puzzled at how the pace of war had slowed.

'This is ominous. They don't seem to be attacking as before. Have they changed their plans?'

'It has proved not an easy task for them to overcome our forces,' Jozow replied. 'It is only a matter of time before they start again. We must be ready.'

His words were prophetic, as fresh attacks commenced, on a larger scale, and with greater frequency. Weight of numbers began to tell in the fierce fighting on the Kurds' much smaller army, whose divisions began the retreat to the foot of the castle.

Khanu tried to strengthen his front line, and to get reinforcements. A squadron of cavalry charged down on the Persian infantry backed by another 300, and from the castle towers the guard saw the approach of a further 500 Kurds. They were a group led by a woman called Zadina Khanim, who sought entry.

'You are our great leader, sir. We are the Malurdan tribe. My husband was killed in war with the Turks. He had no son, so behold, I come to assist our compatriots.'

Khanu and Jozow welcomed them into the castle. Their warriors consisted of both men and women. She was Pestow's cousin. She had gathered her army as soon as she heard that he had been killed in action. She was adamant in bringing women to the fight, as there was no dignity or value for them without their husbands, sons and brothers.

The new army took its position, ready for fresh attacks. The archery division was put at close range, followed by the spears. Persian waves were repulsed one after another, and the fighting remained outside the castle.

The sun began to set over the smoke and carnage. Sardar Khan watched it unfold – the hand-to-hand combat – from one of the mountaintops.

'You cowards, you cowards, don't run away!' Hamza was shouting at the Persians, as Zadina's warriors attacked from left and right. Archers were waiting their opportunity.

A group of women warriors started to sing:

'The mighty God with us,
The mighty God with us.
We won't kneel down
To savages, criminals,
Cursed sons of an evil king.
Brother fight, Heval fight,

With full arms' strength.
War is declared on us,
War is declared on us,
On our Dum Dum Castle,
The symbol of our resilience,
The castle of our freedom,
Of our precious dreams.
With our strong arms,
With our endless patience
Damn the evil king.
The mighty God with us,
The mighty God with us.
We won't kneel down
To savages, to criminals,
To the monstrous Persian king.
The mighty God with us,
The Kurds are bleeding
On rocks, ravines.
In fervent fight,
With swords, spears, gunpowder,
Roar and screams.
Listen to the Persians' wailing corpses.

We fight and fight
With our mountains' dins
To the last man, last drop of blood.
Damn the evil king.

Zadina Khanim's warriors had an immediate impact on the situation, as the weary castle's army had begun to flag. The latest and biggest attack failed under its new leader Sardar Khan.

While Khanu was supervising castle reinforcements, he noted three groups heading towards them, and for that reason withdraw his forces inside, with a few hundred left to guard the ravines and gorges. He called a meeting.

The divan's atmosphere was less euphoric than it had been before, with everyone fully appreciative of the grave situation facing them.

'If the Persian Army was enormous before, it's double that now. We all know very well, this is not going to be easy. They must number at least 40,000. Our destiny depends on how we stand, shoulder to shoulder, brother to brother, sister to sister, resilience the watchword.' He paused. 'I think there is no other way out than to fight. Surrender would be a disgrace, a final humiliation, and we can register no such shameful page in the proud annals of our history. We might just hold out until winter.'

Cheers rang out.

'Our country and nation be proud of us forever!'

'We swear by the honour of our forefathers to protect our castle, to protect our Kurdistan. We are faithful to our leader.'

'Yes, yes, merciful God is our witness,' said Hamza. 'We shall never kneel before the enemy. We shall never know that shame.'

'We die for our country with pride.'

They all knew the one choice they had.

The hustle and bustle of castle life, with its merchants and cattle markets, its caravans and storytellers, turned to gloom and uncertainty, an atmosphere that persisted for weeks and months. Children ceased to play in the alleys. All one saw was preparation for war, with Khanu co-ordinating fortifications for his people. Meanwhile Sardar Khan was looking on.

'What's happening?' he said. 'Have these Kurds been swallowed up in the mountains?' He ordered his command to establish if there were any Kurdish fighters still outside the castle. From afar the castle itself did not seem large enough to accommodate a population of thousands, but close to it was a different matter – the castle was huge, an entire conurbation. Sardar Khan checked on the geographic layout, on the steppes, orchards and woodlands, on the soil and irrigation.

'It's a beautiful country,' he said. 'Well managed. There's no doubt they're a hard-working people.'

'That's right enough, sir. Without that discipline, they wouldn't have been able to build such a castle.'

They searched around for access to it, and in doing so noted no harvesting had taken place.

'That is good,' said Sardar Khan. 'We will not let them collect their crops.'

'It's such a rich land, you can see why they don't

accept anyone's authority over them.'

'They've got it all, yet they don't want to pay taxes to the empire. Well, we'll see about that,' Sardar Khan reflected.

He returned to headquarters and decided on an attack, to which Khanu responded with slingers and rock missiles. They rained down on both sides. Sardar Khan gave the order to attack from a new direction. They attempted to scale the walls with ropes and hooks and wooden ladders, but were foiled, and suffered many casualties in the process. Nevertheless, Sardar Khan forced his slave army ever on, who with no way out were compelled to fight. Still the Kurds resisted.

'Wherever do they get their fighting spirit?' They could not comprehend the Kurdish love of country and community, and their willingness to defend a centuries-old culture. Even their women fought.

After two weeks of fierce battle, Sardar Khan withdrew his army temporarily. He had lost many men, and now he turned his rage to destruction and looting in the surrounding villages. Livestock and field crops were appropriated by the Persian Army.

The situation inside the castle was serious. There was no communication with anyone outside, with other Kurdish tribes ignorant of what was happening to their glorious Dum Dum Castle .

Khanu thought about sending for help, especially from Hakari and Shamdinan, with whom he had very good relations. When the battle restarted, it was relentless, with bombardment around the clock.

Sardar Khan resorted to night attacks, and tried again with ropes and ladders.

§

Dilbar tried to recall the joyous times she had had, when her life was blissful in the bosom of family and friends. She was with her friend Nanie, with whom she shared so many secrets and gossip. She knew the old life couldn't last, and the thought of it made her catch her breath. What of her lover Shabab? Her hands trembled, there was a tightness in her belly. She held a bow in her hand, its leather grip smooth

209

against the touch of her fingers.

Nanie was shooting at the marauders. As she scrambled up towards Dilbar, she caught sight of a bowman fifty paces away. He loosed an arrow. Dilbar hurled herself to the ground, but the shaft had not been aimed at her. She saw Nanie stagger back as her bow fell to the ground, a black-feathered arrow lodged in her chest. Cold fierce anger swept through her. Surging up, she ran to Nanie's side, sweeping up the bow and notching an arrow. The bowman loosed another shaft, which whizzed past her ear. Another scored the skin of her hip. Ignoring the pain, she took aim. The man panicked and tried to get behind a tree, but the arrow thudded into his neck. His legs gave way and he fell.

The woods, mountains and fields around them were in silence. The breeze dropped, and all sounds, the rustle of leaves and bushes, the scurrying of tiny creatures, ceased, as if the world was holding its breath. The moon was huge.

By turns, both men and women stood guard.

Once, when Nanie and Dilbar were on duty, the night was unusually quiet. When morning came, Nanie thought she saw a moving shadow. She alerted Dilbar.

'Don't move. Don't say anything. Someone is coming towards us.'

They stood back and hid in the rocks behind them. There was a man who seemed to crawl as he came towards them. They pounced on and overpowered him, pinning him down. With no hesitation they drew their daggers, threatening to kill him if he moved.

They tied his arms and took him to the divan, where he was interrogated.

He revealed that the two Kurdish warriors Khanu had sent to seek assistance, one of them Khanu's son, had been caught and executed. Three days later the Persians launched another massive attack, again attempting to scale the castle walls, this time with rope ladders, which were soon hacked down, with many falling to their death.

211

Inside was an increasing air of desperation. People gathered, silent and fearful. When an owl hooted, someone remarked on that as a bird of ill omen. The sign was of death and mourning.

Rations were running out, but despite the necessity of further economies no one thought about surrender, even with some of their best men dead. They would carry on for at least six months more, if possible, and hope that with the setting in of winter the siege would end. That decision was in the hands of the enemy, who now had a spy within, a Kurdish tribal leader who had been discovered and detained, guilty of treason. He'd a personal grudge against Khanu, and wanted revenge.

His name was Mahmood Markani, a Kurd, and it had been his intention to show the enemy how to enter the castle. He had once been the miller's assistant, and for years was a livestock trader, and a fine warrior himself. He had fired a written message with an arrow, giving information about the castle's water source, and how to divert it.

'It comes from the north. A tributary from the river passes under a configuration of rocks due north of the castle. That is where to stem the flow.'

He ended with a coded message identifying himself.

The letter was easily picked up, as it was sent in clear morning sunshine. It was delivered to Sardar Khan, who was delighted to read it. He sent a group of men to search for the water source, and to lift away the rocks. When that was accomplished, the water supply was stopped, creating panic in the castle. Now they were dependent on whatever water was stored. Khanu ordered sparing use of it. There was enough for no more than four to five weeks. The only hope now was for autumn rain, but the weeks passed without sign of any.

With supplies low, they considered climbing down to fetch water, but enemy marksmen were waiting. Any who made that attempt would be killed

– it was sheer suicide. Khanu wondered to God what was happening, and how had his people deserved this fate. He was pale and exhausted, with the scar on his cheek enflamed. He called for one last meeting, though most of his leaders were dead. There was no Askander, no Shabab, no Hamza, no Pestow, no Zadina. At the divan the atmosphere had never been so grim. All were weary from shortage of food and water.

'Thank you all for coming tonight, God's peace be on you,' Khanu began. 'Many of you are of our clan, while many more are good friends. It's a day when we appreciate good friends. Survival of the castle is survival of us all. We are all men of war. Sometimes that is a noble pursuit, where death and sacrifice are as glorious as victory itself. We have bent the knee to no one. Each one of you has fulfilled his patriotic duty, and I am proud of every last man, woman, child. Our actions and our resistance will go down in the history of our beloved country.

We have our honour as we face the end, an end

that is not in vain. We pass on to others who follow us the struggle for our country, for our identity. Our scions will carry on the fight, and there *will* be a final victory. I say this when there is no dishonour in surrender, not anymore. I give you that choice rather than fight to the death. I personally will not surrender, but I don't dictate that you should follow suit. I do say this. My last act will be to blow up the castle.'

Khanu stepped down and walked to the balcony.

A young man came forward and spoke for the rest when he declared his support for Khanu's last stand.

'We swear to God we will never surrender. We are with you. We have been your faithful soldiers, and nothing there has changed. We have lived your ideals, and now we die with you, for the glory of our country.'

The decision to detonate the castle was agreed on, with no one willing to surrender. They packed their remaining gunpowder along the walls, in the divan, in the market and in the mosque, and early the next morning it was detonated, with explosions followed by fire. As Khanu's last brave souls met their end a plaint rang out:

'Come on, heval, come on, heval, comrade,
We would die with our castle's demise,
With no surrender.
We declared our intention
Not to be slaves,
So this can't be to anyone's surprise.
We never gave in,
We have known nor shame nor humiliation.
We fought for our country, for Khanu,
And for our dignity,
And we die that the next generation may live.
Let the country, and the mountains,
Let all the civilised world be witness,
Khanu is our great leader.
The castle is our grave, our holy sepulchre,
For there we preferred to die
And not be turned into slaves.
We who fought the Persian and the Turk
Have no blemish on our souls.

The fire raged on for two days, the Persians scarcely able to believe it, and disappointed that they would not now be able to make use of the castle. Quietly they showed their respect for the hundreds of families, men, women and children, who had committed themselves to the flames, with all that was left of them summarised as a pile of debris and a column of smoke.

Sardar Khan ordered a small group to look for any survivors. They found no one alive, but only a scattering of corpses, charred and unrecognisable. Now the looting commenced, with nothing left of any value. Sardar Khan followed them in, and rooted around what was left of the divan and the castle's infrastructure. There were three floors with a multitude of rooms, stone and marble staircases, a rations cache and a weapons dump. He was impressed, and saw much to admire in what was left: arches, vaulted ceilings, fragments of stained glass from the windows, and a few samples of ornamental woodwork. There was evidence of tiled flooring,

217

carpets, rugs and porcelain.

They came across the bodies of two young girls, nineteen or twenty, hanging from a mulberry tree – Nanie and Dilbar. They were adorned in fine traditional dress, and Dilbar had tagged a message to herself:

'We cannot live without our great leader and heroes. Damn the Persian Empire.'

§

The end for Dum Dum Castle came in late November 1609. The villages' crops, orchard fruits, livestock and property generally were plundered, depriving about half a million people. Families, young and old, were either slaughtered or relocated to east and north Iran, though their future generations kept to the same culture, language and tradition.

Shah Abbas unleashed his brutality on innocent villagers and pastoral communities as often he did on his own family and henchmen. He was a cruel dictator whose terrible image is a stain on the history of Kurdistan, Azerbaijan and today Iran.

Epilogue

Resumption of the Iranian wars and suppression of the Celalis

Shah Abbas used peace to centralize his government and build up a substantial army, well supplied with cannon and rifles brought by European technicians, especially the British and French, who were paid and stayed to train his men.

He moved to gain territory, first smashing the Uzbeks and capturing Hart, Mesh and Merv in Transoxania (1588), and after negotiating with Spain and Portugal recapturing Azerbaijan and Caucasus form the Ottomans (1603–04)

Ottoman efforts to resist the Safavid invasion were undermined by lack of discipline and poor leadership. Shah Abbas's capture of Dum Dum Castle and the massacre of its defenders near Lake Urmiya (November 1605) left him in a position to move deeply into eastern Anatolia.

The defeat of the Ottoman Turks also led to the defection of local Turkmans and Kurdish chiefs and a new series of Celali revolts, of which the most

219

serious was led by the Kurdish Junbulat family in northern Syria, Lebanon and most of Cilicia, and by the Kalendergoglu in central Anatolia. (Cilicia = Armenia inhabited by Kurds and Armenians.)

The Celalies were finally crushed in the summer of 1608 by a force under the leadership of kuyucu (the gravedigger) Murat Pasha. All the Anatolian Sancaks were sent more soldiers, and a mass effort was made to hunt down the last of the rebels, with thousands sent to Istanbul as a demonstration of the new order being imposed.